Practical Guide to Toddler Parenting

PRACTICAL GUIDE TO Toddler Parenting

Trusted Strategies for Busy Parents to Raise **Kind** and **Confident Kids**

ZOE CHIEL, PhD

Zeitgeist • New York

Zeitgeist™
An imprint and division of Penguin Random House LLC
1745 Broadway, New York, NY 10019
zeitgeistpublishing.com
penguinrandomhouse.com

ISBN: 9798217151219
Ebook ISBN: 9798217151202

Printed in the United States of America

1st Printing

Book design by Erin Yeung
Cover art © by Daria A/Shutterstock.com
Author photograph © by Batsheva Isser
Edited by Clara Song Lee

The authorized representative in the EU for product safety and compliance is Penguin Random House Ireland, Morrison Chambers, 32 Nassau Street, Dublin D02 YH68, Ireland. https://eu-contact.penguin.ie

To Caleb, Elliot, and Adrian,
with love

CONTENTS

INTRODUCTION

Long before I became a parent, I worked in clinical settings with parents of toddlers and preschoolers. In college, I facilitated parenting groups focused on cultivating strong, secure parent-child relationships while also bolstering parents' abilities to navigate challenging childhood behaviors. I witnessed families transform by building skillfulness and confidence in parenting in a way that was responsive to their children's individual needs and promoted their development. This led me to pursue my doctorate in psychology and to focus my research on the influencing factors of both positive and harmful parenting behaviors.

When I became a parent amid the COVID-19 shutdowns of 2020, I felt overwhelmed by the noise of mixed messages, despite my years of clinical work and research expertise in parenting. I was inundated with seemingly endless parenting content online. Although some of what I saw was validating and supportive, there was also content that contradicted the established research I knew from my background in psychology.

Grounded in the evidence-based knowledge of my clinical and research experiences, I was able to find a path forward in my own life and with my clients. My hope is that through this book, I can share with you my insights from my many years of clinical experience, which have been strengthened by my lived experiences as a parent who continues to find practical ways to apply parenting research to situations in my life.

To all parents who are reading this book, thank you for being here. Parenting can feel overwhelming, whether you have one child or multiple, are a single parent or live in a multigenerational home, or are working multiple jobs or as a stay-at-home parent. For this reason, I encourage all readers to begin with part 1 of this book, which provides information about typical child development, behaviors, and emotions, as well as some practical tools that apply to many situations. With this knowledge, the strategies offered in part 2 will be easier to implement.

Part 2 is a collection of reference guides for raising young children aged 2 to 5, so turn to the sections that you need most at any given stage. Within part 2, chapter 4 will help parents approach common challenges when dealing with typical toddler and preschooler needs, like eating, sleeping, and learning. Chapter 5 addresses specific situations and behaviors that parents may find tricky to navigate, like transitions in childcare, welcoming new siblings, and risky play. Each guide provides insight into both the young children's and parents' perspectives, practical strategies that align with effective parenting behaviors grounded in research, and tools to help parents cope with their own reactions to these challenges.

My hope is that readers will come away with a greater sense of empowerment. There is no cookie-cutter way to parent. Every child is different, and every family is different. I want to help you build a toolbox of options that may work for your family, but I also want you to know that what works best in any given situation depends on many factors. With the confidence you'll gain from understanding early childhood development and gaining practical tools, I hope you'll start to experience less stress—and more joy—in your parenting.

This book is meant to be a digestible resource for toddler and preschooler parents who need a boost of extra support and encouragement and some practical tools. Many topics could be addressed in much greater depth, and fortunately, many wonderful authors and researchers have written those books already. At the end of the book are recommendations for further reading on several topics covered here.

Part 1

Your Parenting Foundation

This first section provides an important foundation for readers who need answers to common challenges associated with parenting toddlers and preschoolers. First, you'll find a basic overview of early child development and common parenting styles and practices. I'll also share some practical tools for parenting toddlers across various situations, including tips for improving caregiver-toddler communication, understanding the "why" behind challenging behaviors, and breaking the cycle of reactive parenting. Finally, I'll share practical advice for raising young kids to be confident, kind, and responsible human beings, with strategies focused on influencing children's behavior and supporting their learning and social-emotional needs.

Chapter 1

What to Know About Raising Young Kids

This chapter provides foundational knowledge to strengthen your understanding of early child development, children's needs, how toddler behaviors affect parents, your role as a parent, and some practical tips for communicating effectively with your toddler. While it might be tempting to jump ahead to the section on specific tips and situations you may be dealing with, these strategies can be used even more effectively when there is a foundational understanding of the science behind your role as a parent and why your toddler may be behaving in challenging or confusing ways.

Our Jobs as Parents

As parents, we wear many hats. Sometimes our primary job seems to be solely survival through basic needs, like feeding. Other times, we may find ourselves wearing a teacher hat, or a disciplinarian hat, focusing on teaching our children specific skills or life lessons. The common thread is establishing a strong, secure attachment with our children so they feel accepted and loved. From this primary place of connection, all the other roles of parenthood fall into place.

Child attachment literature emphasizes that the parent's primary role is to be the "bigger, stronger, wiser, and kind one." This is described in the Circle of Security parenting program, an educational framework that promotes secure attachment relationships between caregiver and child, which establishes a foundation for children's healthy development and learning. It's a balancing act of sorts: Children need to be able to access their parents as a safe, reliable source of comfort, and parents need to support their child's exploration and discovery of the world around them. From this secure relationship, other parenting goals are accessed, like ensuring their child's health, safety, and well-being; preparing them to be engaged learners and ready for adulthood; and transmitting cultural and familial values.

Toddler Parent Goals

The practical aspects of parenting change throughout the different developmental stages, and those first few months and years spent transitioning from newborn to baby to toddler phase are full of significant changes. Stages vary in how enjoyable and rewarding they are for different parents. If you don't like the phase you're in, that's okay—it's just a phase. But getting a handle on the practical aspects of parenting in every stage will help bring you stability and lower your stress in the more challenging ones.

HEALTH AND SAFETY

In the toddler years, parents can proactively plan to promote health, safety, and well-being. From an early stage, try to set and follow eating and sleeping schedules as consistently as possible. This can help you maintain predictability and consistency in your family routines, which is helpful for meeting toddlers' developmental needs. Establish healthy habits early on and prioritize those that promote physical and mental health throughout the child's lifespan.

In this stage, you can also build your village of trusted supporters. This includes friends and family to whom you can turn for social support and guidance, and trustworthy providers in your community, such as primary care doctors and specialists, therapists, community centers, and childcare providers, who can help support your family's well-being.

PREPARE FOR ADULTHOOD

How can parents prepare toddlers for adulthood? Even in the toddler years, there are many strategies that can help teach some of the basics. And you don't have to be an expert in early childhood education to support toddlers' learning at home. Consider the values that are important to you as a parent, and what kind of person you hope your child will be. Children learn through the actions they see modeled by their parents (for better or for worse!). Teach your child by modeling persistence through challenges at home. Praise their efforts over outcomes. Support development of their autonomy and individuality by allowing them to try and fail before you swoop in to assist. Help your toddler learn new skills by exposing them to new experiences and letting them try things that may be a bit outside their comfort zone. From your trusting, secure base, your child will build confidence to learn and explore the world.

TRANSMIT VALUES

We all develop values based on our families of origin, cultural and religious identities, and societal expectations. Some values are easy to identify, while others may be implicit, or beneath the surface. Becoming a parent may bring up questions about what values you want to pass along to your children. If you're co-parenting, it can be empowering to talk with your co-parent about your family values and how you plan to share them with your children. Parents transmit values by modeling desired behaviors (for example, if your family values speaking respectfully, modeling conflict resolution would look like talking through problems in a calm manner at a neutral time rather than engaging in shouting matches in the heat of the moment). You can also model these values for your children by surrounding yourselves with friends, family, and community supports who live by similar values, and by spending your time, money, and energy on experiences that align with the values you want your children to absorb.

Although these goals are helpful to keep in mind, they can't be met in every single caregiver-child interaction. In the 1950s, pediatrician and psychoanalyst Donald Winnicott described "good enough" parenting, emphasizing the importance of parental imperfection in preparing children for an imperfect world. So, consider whether your interactions align with your parenting goals *most of the time*. These goals can be even harder to live by when dealing with the volatile roller coaster of toddler emotions and behaviors, so give yourself some grace. This book is meant to ground you in practical tools that will help you move toward your goals, as research shows that parents who feel competent and effective as parents are less stressed. Less stress, more joy.

It's Wild Being a Toddler

Toddlers go through a transformative amount of growth in just a few years. Think about it: Toddlerhood is a period of development between the highly dependent neediness of infants and babies to the stage where kids build the self-sufficiency required for school. During this time, parents witness tremendous physical and cognitive growth in their kids. As any parent who feels like they are constantly buying the next size shoe for their toddler can attest, many changes are physical and observable, while other developments are more subtle, unfolding beneath the surface.

Amazing Brain Development

Although human brains are constantly developing over time, toddler brains experience what's known as a *sensitive period* for development. During this time, certain brain regions are more malleable and have a stronger ability to learn from experiences. For this reason, development during sensitive periods is largely shaped by the environments where children are raised and the quality of their interactions. Different types of skills tend to mature during different periods. For example, simple, lower-level sensory processes, like observing basic shapes and sounds, develop in the early months after birth, whereas more complex processes, like interpreting others' facial expressions, mature later.

Human brains are built from the bottom up, starting with primal, adaptive functions that ensure survival, like basic, automatic, biological functions and the fight-flight-freeze stress response. Over time, more complex language, cognitive, social, and emotional skills develop, even throughout the teenage years (picture a teenager slamming their bedroom door—even still, teens' emotion regulation capacities are very much under construction). By the early to mid-20s, human prefrontal cortexes have fully matured, resulting in more complex problem-solving and executive functioning abilities. Even though human brains are continuously developing over the first 20-plus years, the rates of development vary during different periods of time. We see some of the most rapid, significant, exciting growth during the sensitive period of the toddler years.

Exciting Growth Spurts

There's good reason why toddlers are notoriously active. As their body continues to grow and change, their movement needs change, too. This is an exciting time for toddlers as they get to start exploring their world, abilities, and interests more thoroughly.

Physical activity is crucial for toddler development. As toddlers get used to their developing bodies, parents can adapt their expectations to support their toddlers' needs appropriately. While toddlers grow and gain new motor skills, parents can welcome clumsiness and falls within reasonable safety limits.

Toddlers often feel excited about their new skills, and sometimes their interest in showing off their new growth outweighs their interest in sleep or sitting still for a meal. You may also notice changes in your toddler's appetite and sleep drive as they go through periodic growth spurts. These physiological changes may in turn impact their behavior (for example, an active toddler who is too excited to eat may be moodier because they are hungry).

Always Learning, All the Time

Think back to a time when you got to explore an entirely new place—maybe a new vacation destination, an exhibit at a museum, or an unnavigated trail in a familiar park. Recall the sense of wonder you may have experienced as you encountered so much newness. Now imagine being a toddler, for whom almost every experience, place, and ability is new. Toddlers' natural curiosity and increasing aptitude to explore that curiosity allows them to test the world like little scientists. Often, this means exploring without any regard for limitations, which may come across as pushing limits and boundaries. This is a normal part of their development and growth. As parents, we can provide support and supervision to direct their curiosities into safe and appropriate channels.

The toddler and preschool-age years can be a wild roller-coaster ride of highs and lows. Take a step back and see if you can join in their childhood sense of wonder, joy, excitement, and curiosity. They need your loving connection to feel safe to explore and to set limits to keep them safe.

Authoritative Parenting in a Nutshell

In the social media era, where content shared about parenting has exploded, parents hear many buzzwords about parenting styles—*authoritative*, *mindful*, *positive*, *gentle*, *conscious*—the list goes on. Authoritative parenting, in particular, has been well established in research literature for decades. While some people use the other terms interchangeably, some of these approaches are more inconsistently defined and lack a research base. In general, the framework of authoritative parenting aligns with the parenting goals of those who want to raise children in a way that:

- Respects the individual needs of the child
- Recognizes that all feelings are acceptable
- Helps their child grow into a responsible, confident adult through the use of developmentally appropriate boundaries and limits

In the 1960s, clinical and developmental psychologist Diana Baumrind described four parenting styles in relation to two different categories of parenting qualities: responsiveness (or warmth) and demandingness (or control). It's important to note that demandingness in this context refers to the use of limits and boundaries. We'll explore this further.

Authoritative parents adopt parenting behaviors that are highly emotionally warm and responsive, treating children as humans deserving of respect, in combination with developmentally appropriate rules, limits, and discipline that foster children's development and growth. Authoritative parenting employs a balance of responsive and demanding qualities. **Permissive parents** are also warm and highly responsive to their child, yet so much so that they often defer to their child's preferences, without setting or enforcing rules or limits, giving children little to no constraints or adult guidance. **Authoritarian parents** lack the warmth and responsiveness that we see in authoritative and permissive parents, while being highly demanding and controlling, focused on requiring children to comply with adults' demands without regard for the child's perspective or needs. Finally, **neglectful or uninvolved parents** show low levels of both demandingness and responsiveness, characterized by a lack of involvement in children's needs or development. Children are left to fend for themselves without the guidance of an adult figure providing the necessary support to foster their growth and development.

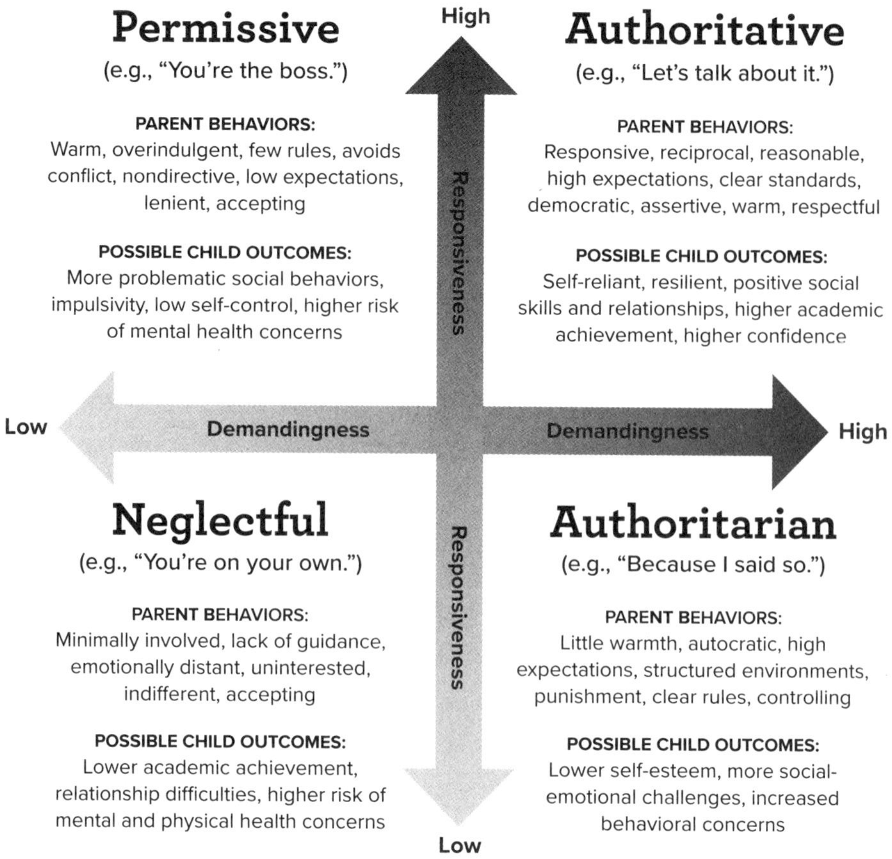

High

Permissive

(e.g., "You're the boss.")

PARENT BEHAVIORS:
Warm, overindulgent, few rules, avoids conflict, nondirective, low expectations, lenient, accepting

POSSIBLE CHILD OUTCOMES:
More problematic social behaviors, impulsivity, low self-control, higher risk of mental health concerns

Authoritative

(e.g., "Let's talk about it.")

PARENT BEHAVIORS:
Responsive, reciprocal, reasonable, high expectations, clear standards, democratic, assertive, warm, respectful

POSSIBLE CHILD OUTCOMES:
Self-reliant, resilient, positive social skills and relationships, higher academic achievement, higher confidence

Responsiveness

Low Demandingness Demandingness High

Neglectful

(e.g., "You're on your own.")

PARENT BEHAVIORS:
Minimally involved, lack of guidance, emotionally distant, uninterested, indifferent, accepting

POSSIBLE CHILD OUTCOMES:
Lower academic achievement, relationship difficulties, higher risk of mental and physical health concerns

Authoritarian

(e.g., "Because I said so.")

PARENT BEHAVIORS:
Little warmth, autocratic, high expectations, structured environments, punishment, clear rules, controlling

POSSIBLE CHILD OUTCOMES:
Lower self-esteem, more social-emotional challenges, increased behavioral concerns

Responsiveness

Low

The chart above illustrates Baumrind's four parenting styles, showing how different levels of responsiveness and demandingness shape the ways we interact with our children. Each approach can be associated with certain developmental outcomes over time—but it's important to remember that parenting is one of many factors that influence a child's development. Wherever your current approach falls on the spectrum, know that your commitment to learning and your care for your child's well-being already speak volumes. If you notice your current parenting behaviors don't fully align with the long-term vision you have for your child or your family, that's okay—awareness is a powerful first step. The goal here is simply to give you a framework to better understand how different parenting behaviors relate to your child's development and your goals as a family, helping you move toward a more authoritative parenting approach.

Take a moment to consider your long-term goals for your children. What kind of person do you want to raise them to become? Kind, considerate, compassionate? Independent, confident, responsible? Resilient? High achieving? Authoritative parenting provides children with a balance of warmth, nurturance, and emotional attunement that is crucial for learning and social-emotional development, as well as limits and expectations that shape children to develop many skills they will need throughout their lives.

The skills and strategies provided throughout this book are consistent with the framework of authoritative parenting. This includes strategies for understanding children's developmental needs, supporting their social-emotional learning, identifying age-appropriate expectations for their behaviors, and implementing firm and consistent limits. Ideally, this is achieved in a way that is warm and responsive to a child's needs, favors connection and communication, encourages autonomy, and sets limits and clear rules that are appropriate for the child's age and developmental level, including discipline techniques that are clear, predictable, rational, and developmentally appropriate.

Conversely, parenting behaviors that are inconsistent with authoritative parenting include psychologically and emotionally harmful behaviors, such as name-calling and shaming; physically harmful behaviors, such as spanking; and neglectful behaviors, such as ignoring children's physical, medical, educational, and/or emotional needs.

For parents who are seeking to break familiar intergenerational patterns of harmful parenting, recognize that your openness to learning new ways of thinking, and new skills, is your superpower. Perhaps you've identified that you were parented in a permissive, authoritarian, or neglectful manner, and you want to parent your children differently but may not have had the models in your life to show you what that looks like. Or maybe you've had generally positive parenting models but want to yell less than what you experienced as a child. Everyone's parenting journey begins at their own unique starting point. And while you approach your parenting with intentionality, remember that change happens gradually. Although you may have a vision of how you want to parent, not every interaction with your child needs to be perfectly aligned with that vision. Allow yourself some grace and patience.

We're aiming for "good enough" parenting, where *most of the time* you are leading with a balance of warmth, responsiveness, and firm guidance. To do this all the time is unrealistic—no parent should put that much pressure on themselves!

Authoritative Parenting Tips for Toddler Caregivers

Authoritative parenting isn't just for toddlers; it's a parenting style that can be applied across the developmental spectrum. While the ins and outs of parenting a toddler may look quite different from parenting a teenager, the key concepts remain the same: maintaining high levels of warmth and responsiveness alongside the use of boundaries and structure that stimulate growth and learning. Naturally, the actual parenting skills and behaviors will look different based on the developmental level of the child.

Here are some quick tips to set up your family for success:

- **Meet your kid where they are.** Be mindful of your toddler's skills and developmental level, as well as day-to-day (or hour-to-hour) variations in mood, sleepiness, and hunger. Adjust your expectations and demands to fit what's realistic for them in that moment or stage.

- **Celebrate your child's strengths.** When you recognize what your child is good at, you can focus consistent responsiveness and positive attention on their most wonderful qualities, and then leverage these strengths to enhance their efforts to grow in other areas.
- **Always consider your child's developmental level and set expectations accordingly.** It's easy to forget that a highly verbal two-year-old has the emotional maturity of . . . a two-year-old. Or perhaps you have a child who struggles to comprehend directions the same way their older sibling did at the same age. Adjusting your expectations to meet your child's developmental needs will benefit everyone.
- **Establish a strong foundation of warm, positive interactions.** Always aim for more frequent positive interactions than criticisms, even if you have to be purposeful or count them at times!
- **Optimize your environment.** Consider how factors in the environment may help with successful outcomes:
    - For example, if you want your child to put on their own shoes, giving your toddler their shoes while telling them to put them on will (1) make it more likely that they will comply, and (2) make the task more accessible for them, supporting development of their emerging independence.
    - Consider how timing and schedules may need to be adjusted. If you encounter nightly conflict transitioning from playtime to bedtime, end playtime a few minutes early, leaving more time for your bedtime routine.
- **Reevaluate, looking for clues to help you respond.** If your toddler reacts with frustration or noncompliance, or ignores you, consider whether they actually have the skills to meet your expectations.

Do they need you to complete the task for them? Do it with them? Show them how to do it more easily?

- **Establish and maintain consistent routines.** As best you can in this busy world, establish consistent routines for daily sleep, mealtimes, and schedule. Predictability is stability. It's easier to set and maintain limits when predictable systems are already in place.
- **Embrace flexibility.** When you can embrace flexibility within your preestablished routines and rituals, it's much easier to hold boundaries. If you eat dinner at 6:00 p.m. but your child is ravenous at 5:00 p.m., offer them a plate of veggies as a predinner snack. This way, they'll still participate in the family mealtime at six, but you'll prevent an escalation from a hangry toddler in the meantime.
- **Hold reasonable boundaries.** Prepare to maintain boundaries with gentle but firm physical interventions when needed.
- **Aim for consistency.** Consistent warmth and responsiveness, as well as consistent rules, expectations, and limits, help establish a secure base from which your child can learn and grow.
- **Express love and enjoyment.** Whether through words or physical affection, expressing your love and enjoyment of your child helps maintain a strong connection, even through the most challenging moments.

I often hear parents express fear that they're "messing up" their kids or wondering, *Am I doing this parenting thing right?* In general, if your child is healthy and safe, and you know that the overall pattern of your parenting tends toward progress and positive growth, you can cut yourself some slack. Not every interaction needs to be a learning moment. When you find yourself fixating on something, ask yourself, *Will there be serious harm if I give my child or myself a little more grace here and just let this go?*

When Caregivers Disagree

The effects of authoritative parenting behaviors are most impactful when both caregivers take this approach. But if one caregiver is struggling to do so, know that having just one secure relationship that lets a child feel safe to explore the world while being held to appropriate limits is still protective for kids in the long term. If you're committed to an authoritative parenting approach, the following strategies offer ways that caregivers can work together to align their parenting styles and practice.

Schedule discussions. Plan a neutral time to talk with your co-parent calmly about each of your perspectives. Often, tangential disagreements can emerge from an argument, and when emotions are running high or you're both just trying to survive a toddler tantrum, it's nearly impossible to have a productive conversation about parenting philosophies.

Find common ground. What are your individual and mutual parenting values? Share and listen to each other's perspectives about how daily parenting behaviors align (or don't align) with your larger goals. Collaborate to find ways that each person's perspective can be acknowledged and to work together toward a shared vision. Offer your perspective on how certain behaviors do or don't align with those goals, and allow your co-parent to offer theirs.

Get specific. What are the specific parenting behaviors that each co-parent finds problematic? Maybe the criticism isn't globally about parenting style, but rather a concern about a specific action. Present the issue through the lens of opportunity rather than criticism. You can do this by addressing agreeable solutions rather than focusing on the problem. It can help to try to connect on shared goals and visions.

continued

Plan ahead. Whether you're co-parenting under the same roof or navigating splitting time between two homes, kids benefit from a consistent parenting approach. When rules, expectations, and consequences change drastically between caregivers, it can create confusion and make it more challenging to support the child's development. Granted, not every caregiver will respond in the exact same way to the same interaction. However, you can come to an agreement on what is absolutely off the table (such as physical discipline and name-calling).

Agree to disagree. Make a plan for how you will handle situations when you disagree. There are many ways to approach a situation, and as long as you've agreed upon what is completely off-limits, make plans that are acceptable to you both for how to approach situations differently.

Experiment, trust, and be open-minded. If the proposed alternate approach isn't harmful but just different, release some control. Trust your partner to try a new approach, and do your best to be open-minded to the outcome. Plan for how you will debrief and move forward.

Consult with a mediator or family therapist for support. When high levels of caregiver disagreement and conflict seem impossible to resolve, consider consulting a specialist who can help co-parents navigate a path forward. Children pick up on the stress of their caregivers, and involving your child in the specifics of parental disagreements can contribute to a loyalty conflict, where children feel confused about their love and trust toward each caregiver. This increases distress and can contribute to behavior problems. Many conflictual co-parenting relationships can be transformed with the support of a specialist (see page 195 for resources).

Toddler Communication Tips

As toddlers' language and communication skills develop, it can be both an exciting and perplexing time for parents learning the nuances of their toddlers' efforts to communicate. Different communication skills develop at different times, and every child is different, so it can sometimes be effortful for parents and toddlers to communicate and understand each other clearly.

Tips to Optimize Communication

- **Check your toddler's battery level.** Consider your child's capacity to take in what you are saying at any given moment. Are they tired, hungry, or in need of a diaper change? Is the environment calm or overwhelming? A child's internal experiences combined with the status of their environment can influence their responsiveness.
- **Pair verbal and nonverbal communication.** When talking to your toddler, consider adding a nonverbal cue like a tap on the shoulder to gain their attention, pointing or gesturing to an item or space you're referring to, or physically bringing an item that you're referring to closer to them. This can help guide their attention to you and what you're communicating.
- **Go little by little.** Watch out for your toddler's limit of how much information they can take in at once, and allow them time to process. Too much information can be confusing and overwhelming. Instead, you might break instructions into two or three parts, only explaining the next step when one step is completed. Offer several seconds of wait time before explaining the next step or repeating yourself. You can do so by counting to five in your head to help pace yourself while giving your toddler time to process.

- **Tell and describe instead of asking.** Asking questions in place of direct instructions can be confusing or lead to power struggles. If you're trying to get your child to follow an instruction, it's better to tell them what to do than to ask—for example, a reasonable answer to the question "Are you ready to leave the playground?" is "No," even if you need to leave! You can also help promote development of their language skills by describing what you observe, rather than asking, as your child might not have the language skills to answer. So, instead of "What are you doing?" try "You're making that car zoom so fast!" Or instead of "What is that?" try pointing and saying, "Wow, I see an airplane in the sky!" This opens the door to a more organic conversation, through which they can express their observations and enthusiasm, too.
- **Expect toddlers to feel frustrated.** Even adults feel frustrated when we're misunderstood! Communication is a developing skill for your child, so unsurprisingly, there will be bumps and feelings of frustration along the way. When that happens, you can channel your warmth and love to support them through it.
- **Consider differences in development.** Different aspects of toddlers' communication abilities may develop at varying rates. This includes their ability to understand (receptive language), share ideas (expressive language), communicate words clearly (articulation), and communicate using both verbal and nonverbal means (like gestures). Your child might have an idea about what they want to share but lack the ability to express the idea clearly. Or your child may be able to understand much more than they can say. Try to be mindful of your child's abilities and limitations, and consult with your pediatrician if you need guidance regarding expectations for your child's language abilities.
- **Be patient.** Recognize that communicating with toddlers requires patience, both for your toddler and yourself. When trying to get you and your toddler from point A to point B, allow yourselves

extra time, and go easy on yourself if you're running a bit late. Trying to rush is stressful for both you and your toddler and can lead to breakdowns in communication.

- **Expect tough moments.** Communicating with toddlers isn't always easy! Forgive yourself when you're not your most patient or skillful self.

Tips to Understand Your Toddler

- **Describe what you see.** If you're struggling to understand your child's words, describe what you see them doing. At a minimum, you are joining their world at their level. It also may help you find a new perspective from which to better understand them.
- **Reflect what you hear.** Even if you can't entirely understand their words, try repeating what you hear. This type of reflection, even if not perfectly accurate, may help your child feel more understood and help them adjust their communication efforts as they try to clarify. Reflecting also helps build toddlers' communication skills through gentle corrections. If a toddler points to their bottle and says, "Buh-buh," you can reflect the correct words back, saying, "Oh, you want your *bottle*. Here you go!"
- **Lean on nonverbal communication.** Ask your child to show you what they are talking about, or try to guess based on body language. If they're standing in the kitchen, you might say, "Oh, you want a snack!" Show them some options that you think they might be looking for, and see how they respond.
- **Ask them to show you.** Prompt your child to show you what they are referring to. Maybe they'll take you with them to another room or have you lift them up to get something that's on a shelf.

- **Guess.** Based on what you know about their needs at that moment (for example, is it close to lunchtime?) or what happened in their day (did they play with a friend they want to tell you about?), see if you can guess some possibilities. Maybe you can narrow down your guess to a few choices. Show or say two choices, and see if it helps clarify.
- **Validate frustration.** Recognize how frustrating it can be to struggle to communicate. Validate for your child ("I know you're feeling frustrated that I can't understand you!"). Also validate your own feelings as the parent. It's okay to feel frustrated or stressed when you can't figure out what your child is trying to tell you. Remind yourself that you are both learning, and this feeling won't last forever. Baby steps.

Tips to Help Your Toddler Understand You

- **Physically get on their level.** Get in close, and squat down to your toddler's eye level so you can look at each other face-to-face. You might give a gentle physical touch on their shoulder to help guide their attention to you.
- **Keep it brief.** Use simple language and short phrases or sentences that match your child's developmental level. Instead of saying, "Please go to the front door and put on your shoes," say, "Shoes on, please!"
- **Keep it simple.** When guiding your toddler to follow through on a task, start with one instruction at a time to avoid pushing the limits of their attention span. Rather than instructing, "Please clean up your toys and go put on your socks and shoes," take it one step at a time. This way, you'll increase the likelihood that your child can (and will) follow through.

- **Check your tone.** Use a calm, neutral tone when delivering explanations or instructions or setting limits (even if you're feeling impatient or frustrated!). Use an enthusiastic tone to emphasize and celebrate positive behaviors and interactions. By using a calm and appropriate tone for different situations, you help your child understand the intention of your message. You're also modeling effective communication for them to use as they grow!
- **Start with an explanation.** Before giving a direction to your child, explain the rationale. For example, "It's time to go pick up your sister from school. Please get your shoes." When you start with an explanation, you're less likely to get pushback because your child will understand why they're being told what to do. When you end with the instruction, the child has more time to process and follow through on the task because it's the most recent piece of information they heard.
- **Frame actions positively.** Tell your child what to *do* instead of what *not to do.* Instead of "Don't yell," try "Please use your calm and quiet voice." You can also start with an explanation, such as "The library is a quiet place. Please use your calm and quiet voice."
- **Ensure understanding.** If your child has the language skills to do so, allow them to repeat the plan to ensure understanding. You can do this playfully by making it a fill-in-the-blank game. After talking them through a plan, start repeating the plan and pause throughout to allow your toddler time to fill in the blank: "It's time for . . . That's right, dinner! First, we're going to . . . Yes, wash your hands. Then we will . . . sit at the table and get ready to . . . eat! Hooray!"
- **Tell, don't ask.** When an instruction is not optional, tell your child what to do, instead of asking or suggesting. Let's say you want your child to sit in their chair for lunch. Instead of asking, "Are you ready to sit at the table?" to which they can answer, "No," or

suggesting, "Let's sit at the table now," which sounds optional and like something you are doing together, try "Please come sit in your chair."

- **Be playful.** Use a stuffie or doll to talk to your child or model what you want to communicate to your child. Like, "Doggy, it's time for Jane to brush her teeth! First, we put toothpaste on her toothbrush. Thanks for helping me, Doggy! Hmm, now what's next?"
- **Offer behavior-specific praise.** When caregivers praise their child for specific behaviors, they are more likely to engage in those behaviors in the future. A compliment like "Thank you for listening right away!" will help shape your child's listening skills.

Frequently Asked Questions

Why isn't my toddler talking nearly as much as their cousin did at the same age?

Remember that aspects of language develop at different paces for different kids. Home in on your child's communication strengths and difficulties. You can help by modeling language use throughout your day: Narrate what you are doing with your toddler, read books aloud, and engage in interactive play to help bolster language skills. If you have concerns about your child's language development, consult with your pediatrician.

My toddler has begun saying no or doesn't listen whenever I give an instruction. What should I do?

Try to identify the "why." If you can identify the reason behind "not listening," it will be easier to resolve. See "Decoding Difficult Behaviors," pages 35–43, for some suggestions under the issues "Always saying no/refusing to try new things" and "Ignoring/not following directions."

How do I communicate when my child won't stop screaming or crying, even after an hour or longer?

Even when it seems endless, I promise, crying and screaming will eventually stop. For many kids, too much talking can be overstimulating (even talking about feelings and soothing strategies). Focus on physical regulation strategies, like stepping outside for fresh air and temperature change, or rinsing off in a bath or with a cool washcloth. Call for backup from another caregiver, when possible. Try your best to keep your manner calm and collected to remain a sturdy, soothing presence. You've got this!

My child recoils from my touch when I try to soothe them. How should I respond?

As long as your child is physically safe, you can respect the boundary they are setting while also letting them know that you're available when they need you. Avoid getting too focused on the way they are acting—coming from a place of emotion dysregulation, they may feel overstimulated. You might say, "It seems you want a little space. I will be right over here if you need me." It's okay to allow your child some personal space—just keep a close eye out so you can step in when they're ready.

Decoding Difficult Behaviors

As toddlers follow their sense of curiosity to learn about the world, they will explore in ways that you, as a fully formed adult, know to be unsafe, irritating, or problematic. But as completely new learners, toddlers try all sorts of behaviors—some that are okay, and some that are not! It's important to remember that we're not born knowing right from wrong. Kids learn which behaviors are and are not acceptable by observing how adults respond to their exploration and limit testing and watching how other people in their world behave. It may reassure you to know that many challenging behaviors are actually a sign of healthy, normative development. Behavioral control skills and self-regulation develop through experiential learning and brain development over time.

Just because many of these behaviors are considered normal doesn't mean it's easy for us parents to handle! We can find it helpful to understand what is developmentally appropriate and the different reasons why these behaviors might occur. Knowing the *why* behind a behavior can help us decide how to respond. Some parents may also find it helpful to recognize when and how these difficult behaviors may be triggering an internal response for the parent, which is sometimes rooted in one's own personal experiences, upbringing, and history. We'll explore this in chapter 3.

Generally, when toddlers don't have the words or skills to express their internal feelings, they express themselves through actions. I offer suggestions to encourage you to think about the possible reasons behind your child's difficult behaviors. It can help to remind yourself that your toddler's difficult behaviors are part of their learning and growing; they're not intentionally misbehaving, manipulating, or provoking you. If you notice an instinct to assume bad intentions, ask yourself, *Why else might they be acting this way?* This can provide you with an opportunity to reframe their behavior in the context of normative (albeit challenging!) toddler development.

The following are some challenging toddler behaviors. For each behavior, I list common reasons why they might happen and strategies for how parents can respond.

Biting (nonaggressive)

COMMON REASONS:

- **Self-soothing**

  Strategy: Redirect to appropriate teething toy for self-soothing

- **Playfulness or affection**

  Strategy: Redirect to appropriate alternative (such as closed-mouth kiss)

- **Task frustration**

  Strategies:

  - Label it: "Ouch, that hurts."
  - Redirect to alternate action to express frustration
  - Coach emotion regulation (see "How to Soothe and Support," page 87, and "Co-Regulation to Self-Regulation," page 83)
  - Assist with the task causing frustration

- **Difficulty communicating**

  Strategies:

  - Redirect
  - Coach emotion regulation (see "How to Soothe and Support," page 87, and "Co-Regulation to Self-Regulation," page 83)
  - See "Toddler Communication Tips," page 27

Aggressive behaviors (hitting, pushing, throwing, etc.)

COMMON REASONS:

- **Sensory need**

  Strategies:

  - Set a boundary: "No hitting."
  - Redirect to an appropriate physical activity to meet the sensory need

- **Attention seeking**

  Strategies:

  - Set a boundary: "No hitting."
  - Underreact: Briefly remove attention from child if no one's at risk of harm
  - Redirect to alternate activity
  - Praise appropriate behavior enthusiastically: "Thank you for playing gently!"

- **Difficulty communicating**

  Strategies:

  - Label emotion: "It's so frustrating that the blocks fell!"
  - Physically block child from continuing aggressive behavior

- **Emotion dysregulation**

  Strategy: See "How to Soothe and Support," page 87

- **Exploring environment**

  Strategy: Redirect to alternate behavior: "Fork stays on table or in mouth. After dinner, we can throw a ball."

Screaming and whining

COMMON REASONS:

- **Attention seeking**

  Strategies:

  - Underreact: Briefly remove attention from child
  - Redirect to alternate behavior: "Please use calm words."
  - Give enthusiastic praise for appropriate behavior

- **Difficulty communicating**

  Strategies:

  - Label emotion: "I know you're feeling frustrated."
  - Model appropriate alternate behavior
  - See "Toddler Communication Tips," page 27

- **Physical pain or discomfort**

  Strategies:

  - Assist in soothing and solving the problem (see "How to Soothe and Support," page 87)
  - Label and validate emotion: "I'm sorry that hurts."

- **Frustration; not getting what they want**

  Strategies:

  - Selective attention: Underreact to the whining, and praise appropriate alternate behaviors (like taking a deep breath to cope)
  - Label emotion: "I'm sorry you feel sad."
  - Assist in soothing and solving the problem (see "How to Soothe and Support," page 87)
  - Model appropriate alternate behavior

Clinginess or separation fears

COMMON REASONS:

- **Underprepared for new environment or situation**

  Strategies:

  - Prepare in advance
  - Plan for how child can cope or who the child can ask for help
  - Reassure child that they will be safe (ex., that their babysitter is kind and will take good care of them)

- **Feeling scared or worried**

  Strategies:

  - Prepare in advance
  - Plan for how child can cope or who the child can ask for help
  - Reassure child that they will be safe (ex., their friend's house is a safe place to play)
  - Praise for small steps toward bravery/separation

- **Child's temperament**

  Strategy: Adjust expectations to align with the child's needs

- **Low "connection reserve" (in need of more caregiver attention and connection)**

  Strategies:

  - Plan for daily one-on-one parent-child connection time (see "Fill Connection Reserves," page 53)
  - Use PRIDE skills to increase confidence and connection (see "Fill Connection Reserves," page 53)

Always saying no/refusing to try new things

COMMON REASONS:

- **Asserting independence/personal preference**

  Strategy: Offer choices within limits

- **Testing limits**

  Strategy: See "How to Maintain Your Boundary," page 74

- **Fear or anxiety**

  Strategies:

  - Prepare in advance
  - Plan for how child can cope or who the child can ask for help
  - Reassure child of safety
  - Praise for small steps toward bravery/separation

- **Experiencing limited agency/autonomy/control in daily routines**

  Strategies:

  - Increase sense of control in daily routine
  - Offer two choices
  - Allow child to choose order of events
  - Praise flexibility

Ignoring/not following directions

COMMON REASONS:

- **Does not comprehend or hear instructions**

  Strategies:

  - Rephrase to more developmentally appropriate language

- Get physically close to gain child's attention before instructing
- Adjust the environment to set up for success (ex., move toy bin closer during cleanup)

- **Does not have the skills to complete the task**

  Strategies:

  - Adjust the expectation to a more developmentally appropriate level
  - Offer assistance to complete the task together

- **Know they can get away with ignoring, due to inconsistent follow-through by caregivers giving instructions**

  Strategies:

  - See "How to Maintain Your Boundary," page 74
  - Prioritize follow-through
  - Assist with the task if needed
  - Give enthusiastic praise: "Thank you so much for listening!"

- **Does not want to transition from preferred to less preferred activity**

  Strategies:

  - Offer simple explanation
  - Use task or time strategies to ease transitions: "Dinner's almost ready. In five minutes, after this game, we'll set the table."
  - Rephrase with when/if-then statement: "If you put the trucks in the bin, then you may choose the music in the car."
  - Give enthusiastic praise: "Thank you so much for listening!"

Jumping, climbing, risky play

COMMON REASONS:

- **Exploring and curious**

  Strategies:

  - Physically intervene to ensure safety (ex., grabbing them before they climb onto a pile of unsteady rocks)
  - Redirect to alternate physical behavior (ex., show where to climb instead)

- **Lack of awareness of what is safe and unsafe**

  Strategies:

  - Physically intervene to ensure safety (ex., grabbing them from running into the street)
  - Show them why something is unsafe: "The road has cars. You could get hurt."
  - Redirect to alternate physical behavior (ex., show where to run instead)

- **Attention seeking**

  Strategies:

  - Redirect the child to a more appropriate activity: "We don't climb at the library. Let's do a puzzle."
  - Underreact: Briefly remove attention if no danger is posed
  - Give enthusiastic praise for appropriate behavior

- **Temperament/high activity level and sensory needs**

  Strategies:

  - Physically intervene to ensure safety (ex., stopping them from jumping on a table)

- Redirect to alternate physical behavior (ex., show where to jump instead)
- Give enthusiastic praise for appropriate behavior

Laughing when scolded

COMMON REASONS:

- **Discomfort, embarrassment, shame**

  Strategies:

  - Label emotion: "Sometimes kids feel embarrassed when they hurt someone."
  - Limit caregiver attention on laughter
  - Redirect caregiver attention to appropriate behavior: "Let's check on your brother to see if he's okay."

- **Attention seeking**

  Strategies:

  - Underreact: Briefly remove attention
  - Model and support child in corrective action to what they were scolded for
  - Provide enthusiastic praise for appropriate behavior: "Great job keeping your hands to yourself."

- **Amused**

  Strategies:

  - Underreact to or ignore the laughing
  - Redirect or distract to corrective action

Shyness, hesitation

- **Temperament**

  Strategies:

  - Adjust caregiver expectations
  - Prepare ahead with simple explanations about what to expect
  - Label and validate feelings: "I know you feel shy. It's okay."
  - Find a smaller step toward brave participation
  - Model behavior you want to see (ex., introduce yourself to others and engage enthusiastically)
  - Give enthusiastic praise for small steps of engagement

- **Unsure about what to expect or what is expected of them**

  Strategies:

  - Label and validate feelings: "I know you feel nervous. It's okay."
  - Prepare ahead with simple explanations about what to expect
  - Encourage them in advance: "There are toys you love, like puzzles and trains. Johnny likes puzzles, too!"

- **Lacks skills to appropriately engage (ex., entering a new social situation, unsure how to join peers in play)**

  Strategies:

  - Practice at home with role-playing (ex., playing games, playing with toys)
  - Start small, such as short one-on-one playdates
  - Coach them on what they can say to join in play

Breaking the Cycle of Reactive Parenting

All parents have reactive moments. Your child cries and throws their shoes instead of putting them on when you're scrambling to get out of the house for school, and you shout. They drop food on the floor for the 10th time while looking at you straight in the face, saying, "Oops," and you explode.

It's completely normal to experience a reaction in response to your toddlers' tears, tantrums, and yes, defiance. Actually, it's evolutionarily adaptive! As humans, we're wired to respond to our kids' cries with alarm—it activates our automatic response to attend to their needs. Toddlers in particular are very dependent on their caregivers (despite their protests for independence), and we need to be responsive to those cries for the sake of human survival. At the same time, it's completely normal to feel stress, anger, frustration, or fear in reaction to your child's behavior. How you respond to your own feelings is key. If those reactive moments are a frequent pattern, it's worth taking a closer look at what is happening for you and how you can gain more control over your reactions to shift that balance toward more proactive approaches to parenting.

Perhaps your child's cries remind you of times you were shamed in your childhood, or maybe your uncertainty about how to help your child cope reminds you of the loneliness you felt when your caregivers dismissed your feelings. As parents, we may lose our cool by yelling, blaming, name-calling, or shutting down. All these counterproductive responses are also much quicker to show up when we're feeling stressed, sleep deprived, undernourished, socially neglected, or dealing with our own mental health challenges. This is because humans are wired to revert to a reactive, automatic-stress-response mode when a threat is detected in the environment, and it's physically impossible to access the rational, skillful parts of the brain when this level of distress is present.

Shifting the balance from reactive to proactive or intentional approaches to parenting takes work, but a little bit of intention every day can go a long way. Here are some tips and bits of wisdom:

- **Put on your oxygen mask first.** Do something every day with the intention to take care of yourself. Check out resources on mindfulness (see page 196) to incorporate mindful moments into your daily routine. Something as simple as finding a more intentional way to drink your morning coffee or taking a mindful shower can give you a boost of peace that will carry over throughout your day.
- **Take care of your body.**
  - Try to make time for exercise, and when you can't, find time for daily movement, even if that means parking at the far end of the parking lot to give yourself a little extra walk.
  - Eat nourishing meals—scraps of your kid's leftover mac and cheese don't count.
  - Prioritize sleep. Yes, this can seem impossible when your post-kid's-bedtime to-do list is endless, or when your child has reverted to waking up 10 times in the middle of the night. Yet sleep is essential for refueling your tank. Recognize when this need is impossible to fill, and make sure to give yourself extra grace the next day. Continue to prioritize it when you can.
- **There's no such thing as a perfect parent.** They don't exist. Kids thrive with "good enough" parents.
- **Mistakes are for learning.** This is true for toddlers, and it's true for parents, too. When you react to your toddler in a way that you later regret, take note. Offer yourself compassion. You're doing the best you can with the resources you have at any given moment. Consider how the more regulated, skillful version of yourself would

have handled that situation. Plan for how to make it easier to bring in that version of yourself next time.

- **Repair and recover.** Reactive parenting moments are an opportunity to model for your child how to repair and recover in relationships. This may mean looking them straight in the eye, apologizing, accepting responsibility for your actions, and reminding them that you always love them. Doing and teaching this is a tremendous gift. Everyone will encounter conflict in their lives, and if you can show your child that connection lasts despite conflict, you are equipping them with resilience skills that will last a lifetime.

Chapter 2

Taking a Practical Approach

Many parents seek out parenting books and other resources with the intention to parent differently than how they were parented. In my practice, I often hear parents say, "I know I don't want to yell/spank/threaten/isolate like my parents did, but I'm not sure what to do instead."

In this chapter, you'll learn practical tools that align with authoritative parenting. You'll also explore the foundational skills that foster a strong, secure parent-child relationship and learn how, with that stable foundation, it's easier to set limits and for kids to learn. But again, not every interaction with your child needs to be a teachable moment. With the following framework of authoritative parenting and a toolbox of skills at your disposal, you'll find what works for you and your family, use the tools when you can, and accept the moments when you need to give yourself some grace.

Cover Basic Needs First

As parents, we're responsible for setting up our children for success by creating environments and routines that support their needs. Basic physiological needs contribute significantly to children's development and well-being. It's no surprise that when toddlers are well rested, nourished, have had sufficient daily movement, feel socially connected, and are able to exert autonomy, it's easier to help them regulate their behavior and learn. Chapter 4 will offer more specific guidance on how to meet these needs and the associated challenges.

Tips for Predictable Structure

Children find comfort in predictability and familiarity. With consistent routines, children often experience a greater sense of stability and control in their environment. Even as adults, we can relate to the experience of finding comfort in knowing what's on our schedule each day. Routines can also help our body feel more regulated, in contrast to the discomfort we experience when we're uncertain about what's coming next.

Providing consistent routines and schedules for your family and toddler can make parenting easier. From the parents' perspective, it reduces your mental load by increasing automaticity and familiarity in your daily life. From the child's perspective, it provides a sense of safety and security in knowing what's coming. Although it may be effortful upfront to establish routines that work for your family, with consistency over time, many parents find that their households run more smoothly. And when you need to deviate from your routine—which we know happens—your child will be able to recover much more flexibly afterward because they're resetting back to a familiar routine.

Here's how you can provide predictable structure:

- **Be consistent.** Commit to a routine and try to be consistent with the order of tasks for each period of the day, too. This will make it easier for toddlers to follow through on each step.
- **Offer flexibility within constraints.** Dinner might not happen at the same time every night. That's okay. Know your limits and allow time flexibility within those parameters while maintaining the order of events as well as possible.
- **Demonstrate routines with toys.** Through play, model how a stuffed animal or doll follows a routine that you're helping your child learn to follow, like getting ready for school.
- **Be consistent in routines across caregivers** (such as two households, daycare, etc.) as much as reasonably possible. Kids feel much more stable and secure transitioning between environments when there is some familiarity, even despite some differences.
- **Use transitional comfort objects.** A stuffed animal that travels between home and daycare, or two of the same stuffies for each sleep place, can cue your child to feel comfort and ready for rest.
- **Prepare for transitions between activities.**
    - Rather than a "five-minute warning," younger kids benefit from more concrete transition warnings. For example, "It's almost time to leave the playground. Choose one more thing to play before we go," or "Playtime is almost over. You have time to build three more blocks before cleanup."
    - A visual timer, combined with your reminders, can show kids how much time is left to finish an activity before moving to the next. Note this is more helpful for slightly older kids, as kids must remember to look at the timer to know what's coming.

- Involve kids in setting an audio timer. "Siri/Alexa, please set a one-minute timer!"
- Manage expectations. Tell your toddler when they can expect something to happen in the future. Kids struggle to understand time and permanency. They might wonder, *If I stop playing with these trucks now, will I ever get to play trucks again?* Offer reassurance by reminding them that they will get to enjoy these activities again soon.

- **Talk about what to expect.** Talk about expectations in advance in clear, simple terms, especially when you are establishing new routines. Try using first-then statements ("First we will eat dinner, then we will get ready for bed").
- **Prepare for changes in routine**, when possible. When routines are going to change, whether temporarily, like for a holiday, or permanently, like for a daycare schedule change that has a new morning routine, prepare your child in advance by talking about what they can expect.
- **Use visual reminders.** Toddlers are concrete learners and benefit from visual reminders about routines. You can create a visual schedule, which uses pictures to depict daily activities. Each activity is presented on an individual card—this could be a picture or illustration of the activity, or you can personalize it with photos of your own child and environment. Use these cards with your child to develop an order of activities and routines.
- **Establish co-parenting expectations.** In a two-parent household, plan ahead to assign household tasks to each parent so daily tasks fit into the routines more smoothly. Some parents re-delegate tasks each day, week, month, or even longer term. Find what works for you. (Eve Rodsky offers many practical solutions to sharing household responsibilities in her book *Fair Play*.)

Tips to Help Your Kid Move Their Body

Daily movement is a key component of child development, and kids love it! Benefits of daily physical activity include physical health, motor skill acquisition, cognitive and social development, and sleep quality. Although all children benefit from daily movement, some children have a greater need for activity and sensory input. You can encourage daily movement even when time, space, and resources are limited. Here are some practical tips for promoting your toddler's daily movement.

HOME ACTIVITIES

- **Play music and have a toddler dance party.** Add a challenge with Freeze Dance, pausing the music intermittently and shouting, "Freeze!" This also helps kids practice body control.
- **Create safe spaces for jumping.** Lay the couch cushions on the floor or clear the area around the couch or bed and allow kids to jump.
- **Run and crash.** Create a pile of pillows in an open area and allow kids to run and crash into the pile. For kids who like rough play, this is a great way to show them when and how to safely channel that energy.
- **Build an obstacle course.** Use materials you have at home to create an obstacle course for kids to move through (for example, hop over the toy car, crawl under the table, stand on one foot on the paper).
- **Go wild with animal movements.** Invite them to hop like a frog, strut like a giraffe, or run like a puppy when transitioning between home activities or spaces.

- **Engage in household tasks.** If your child needs extra movement and likes to help, give them a simple, nonessential task that keeps them moving, such as bringing you something from another room.

TIPS WHEN OUT AND ABOUT

- **Encourage walking.** Even when out for a stroller walk, offer opportunities for your toddler to walk independently where safe. If time allows when running errands, allow your child to walk next to you while you push the cart. Just make sure to set the expectations about staying together. Offer a ride in the cart or stroller when they (or you) need it.
- **Bring fidget toys.** When kids are expected to stay seated calmly for a while, like on long car rides, at restaurants, or in places of worship, bring quiet toys to occupy their hands, like squishy stress balls. The fine motor activity will still keep their body (and mind) engaged and moving.
- **Take a shake break.** Wherever you are, give your toddler a chance to release energy with a shake break, where they can shake or wiggle their body while counting to 10.

Tips to Give Kids a Sense of Autonomy

Toddlers love autonomy and independence. One of the key tasks of authoritative parenting in the toddler years is to provide parental support for autonomy development with the right dose of help or facilitating toddlers' use of their own skills. Supporting a toddler's autonomy promotes the development of their problem-solving skills and executive functioning. When we find ways to offer our children choices and opportunities for autonomy, it makes it easier for them to comply when we need to take full control. Here are some practical tips that you can use to give your toddler a sense of control without compromising your schedules and decision-making.

- **Create unstructured playtime.** Establish a designated space that is fully toddler-proof so your child has full control of what and how they play. Even if you don't have space at home for a completely toddler-proof room, use physical boundaries like play mats to designate a free play space.
- **Connect through play.** By balancing their independent playtime with child-led playtime with a primary caregiver, your toddler's autonomy cup will be fuller, and it'll be easier for them to comply when you need to take the lead (see page 54).
- **Offer choices.** Let your little one choose how they will fulfill your desired outcome. You might say, "You choose: Do you want to put on your shirt first or your pants?" or "It's dinnertime! Do you want your milk in the blue cup or red cup tonight?"
- **Involve them in household tasks.** With their drive for both autonomy and social connection, many toddlers love to be helpers. Invite your toddler to help cut soft veggies with a child-friendly knife or put plates on the table.
- **Model the desired behavior.** You can model or use toys to demonstrate a task, such as "Who's going to brush their teeth first, Quinn or the bunny? Great job, bunny! Now it's Quinn's turn!"

Fill Connection Reserves

Children are more responsive to limits being set when there's a strong, connected caregiver-child relationship. All kids want to feel seen, heard, and loved (don't we all?). A core component of almost all early childhood therapeutic interventions—whether to address concerns related to family stress, childhood anxiety or irritability, adjustments to changes at home, or behavioral concerns—is bolstering the connection between caregiver and child through positive attention and connectedness through play. With a stronger relational foundation, we can more effectively and proactively help children problem-solve and cooperate, while strengthening their self-esteem, attachment, and social skills. Consider this analogy to a bank deposit: The more you build your bank reserves, the easier it is to make a withdrawal. When we increase positive attention and connection, our children tend to show less difficult behaviors. When those challenging behaviors do arise, we can use our positive attention and connection skills to shape those behaviors and help them learn. And when we do need to use consequences to influence behaviors, the discomfort of consequences—for both parent and child—is much more tolerable. (We'll discuss this more in "Consequences," page 65.)

Parent-child interaction therapy (PCIT) is a short-term evidence-based treatment approach that helps parents better manage challenging behaviors in young children. This approach promotes the daily practice of "special time," which uses specific skills to enhance the parent-child relationship through play. Through five minutes of daily special playtime, parents use PRIDE skills (see below) to follow the child's lead and connect through play. Even if you're with your toddler all day, every day, the quality of this five-minute special playtime is different from your other interactions.

Here's how it works:

1. **Give it a name.** Whether it's Daddy-Riley time, Special Time, or something else, give this five-minute session a name that will distinguish it from other types of play.

2. **Set the scene.** Choose a space with limited distractions (leave your devices in another room!). Bring two or three choices of open-ended, noncompetitive toys into the play space (such as building blocks, dolls, cars). The caregiver chooses the options; the child

chooses from those options. If you don't have the bandwidth to clean up finger paint, don't offer finger paint!

3. **Take turns with siblings.** Though it might be hard for siblings at first, at least until they see how special time plays out each day, try to have them play with something else during this time to make sure it is just between you and one child. If a sibling shows an interest in special time, you can plan an exclusive time for them while your toddler naps or is otherwise occupied.

Remember the acronym PRIDE to focus on positive attention while following your child's lead during this playtime:

- **Praise behavior.** Turn your attention to the behaviors you want to encourage. This positive attention will encourage your child to repeat that behavior in the future, will strengthen connections in your relationship, and will model positive social skills. For example: "Thanks for sharing the doll!" or "Nice job using kind words."
- **Reflect.** Repeat or paraphrase what your child says, even if they're not forming full words. Reflecting speech shows that you're connected and engaged, encourages kids to express more, and models correct pronunciation to support language development. For example, if your child says "Bok," you can reflect: "Yes, a block!"
- **Imitate play.** Imitate your child's play behaviors to show that you're interested in their play, to help you follow along with their interests and ideas at their level, and to model reciprocal social interactions. For example, if your child races a car, you race a car, too.
- **Describe behavior.** Describe your observations of your child's actions to help maintain connection and attention. This also helps your child stay focused on a task, build self-regulation skills, and learn connections between words and actions. For particularly active children, who might typically play by first dumping out a bin

of blocks, then running to grab a doll, then jumping on the couch, descriptions can help them slow down by keeping their attention engaged on one action at a time. For example, "You're laying out the blocks. Now you're sorting them. You picked up a blue block. Now you found a red one, too!"

- **Enjoy.** Use words and physical affection to express enjoyment of your time together, emphasizing positive emotions and warmth in the relationship. For example, say, "I'm having so much fun playing with you!" while giving them a hug and smiling together.

Questions, commands, criticism, or negative talk from adults can add demands or pressure to playtime, or shift the balance toward too much negative attention. During special playtime, remember to:

- **Minimize questions.** This can be hard to resist! While this is an intuitive way that many caregivers engage in play, even a simple question like, "What are you building?" can interrupt the play, take away the child's lead, or feel overwhelming if the child doesn't know the answer or have the language skills to respond.
- **Avoid commands.** Children receive many commands throughout their day when their adults need to be in charge. Even when they're intended to engage, adult commands can elicit negative interactions or take over the direction of the child's play; for example, "Let's build a tower" or "Look at this car."
- **Cut out criticism or negative talk.** Words like *no*, *don't*, *stop*, *quit*, and *not* should be avoided during special playtime (except in response to a dangerous behavior). Instead, build up that reserve of positive interactions. Ignore minor, harmless misbehaviors, like screaming, and focus your attention on finding opportunities to use PRIDE skills, like "You're picking up the doll" (description) or "Thank you for sitting on the play mat" (praise).

Quick Tips for Increasing Positive Attention and Connection Throughout the Day

PRIDE skills and positive attention can happen throughout the day, too! Make space for these easy ways to connect positively with your child:

- Share compliments. Offer behavior-specific messages of praise to your child throughout the day. ("Wow, good job!" "Thanks for picking up your toy!" "I love how you're taking turns.")
- Allow your toddler to overhear you complimenting them. Whether talking to your co-parent, on the phone, or even dictating a text message to another parent or grandparent in the presence of your child, talk about what you love about them to someone else. This is a great strategy for parenting children of any age!
- Tell your child how much you enjoy your time with them.
- Even if you can't set aside five minutes for daily special playtime, try to use the PRIDE skills in other parts of your routine, like bathtime or mealtimes. These skills promote positive parent-child interactions, keeping both your and your child's connection cups full.

Manage Your Expectations

Most parents come into parenting without much knowledge of child development or what to expect. Managing expectations for our children can feel like a Goldilocks problem: When expectations are too low, parents intervene too soon and inadvertently interfere with children's growth; when expectations are too high, both kids and parents are left feeling frustrated and confused by mismatched standards. Much like the "just-right porridge," when we have an awareness of general developmental expectations, we are better able to facilitate our children's growth by responding to their needs appropriately and in a way that aligns with goals of authoritative parenting. It also results in less stress and frustration when we know what behaviors are developmentally appropriate and can set reasonable expectations for ourselves and our children.

Although every child is different, it helps to know what to expect from an average child at any given stage. Individual differences like temperament, activity level, sensory needs, and adaptability (and how these individual differences align or may differ between parent and child) can contribute to a wide range of appropriate expectations at a given stage.

Ages 1 to 2 Years

This second year of life is an exciting time for both caregivers and toddlers. Typically, toddlers are much more mobile and able to explore their environment more independently, making them curious and socially engaged—they may be excited to show you a toy that interests them. Although they can get around more independently, toddlers at this stage still have so much to learn about the world and don't have an understanding of how to engage with different materials and spaces safely. They need our guidance and supervision to intervene and teach them how to interact with their environment safely. It's important to provide safe spaces where they can move and explore freely.

Toddlers' language generally develops rapidly during this time. At this stage, they may start associating your words with gestures and materials. Consider how you use both verbal and nonverbal language to bolster their language, such as saying, "Look, a fire truck!" while pointing.

Toddlers are just starting to learn associations between cause and effect. They may not realize that putting a ball on a slope will cause it to roll (and may become frustrated when their toys don't stay in place). Tantrums are also normal at this stage. Give your toddler time and space to calm down. Use the tools from "How to Soothe and Support" on page 87 to co-regulate and teach them to soothe.

Ages 2 to 3 Years

At this stage, a toddler's cognitive and social growth tends to be expansive. While still highly reliant on caregivers to get needs met, their drive for independence and control increases, and they may exert that desire for control through frequent use of the word *no*. Toddlers at this stage start to develop greater ability to regulate the broad range of emotions they experience, yet they will still need caregiver support to develop emotion-regulation skills (for years to come!).

Many two-year-olds seem like they are constantly on the go. Their need for more movement may make it harder for them to sit still to listen to a book or eat a meal than it was just a few months ago. While often frustrating for parents, this is totally normal. Allow for the busy energy of a two-year-old who seems to constantly move from one thing to the next.

Language development expands rapidly. At the age of two, children typically understand much of what is said to them and begin putting multiple words together to form sentences and ask questions. However, communication can be frustrating, as some two-year-olds may struggle to articulate words intelligibly for all to understand, or may lack the words they need to express their thoughts. On the flip side, parents of toddlers with more advanced language skills can forget that having advanced expressive language skills doesn't mean that their toddler is capable of regulating emotions and behaviors in the same advanced way.

Emotionally, kids at this stage become more aware and curious about others' emotions, noticing when peers are crying or checking parents' faces for reactions to unfamiliar situations.

Ages 3 to 4 Years

Between ages three and four, the typical toddler is becoming more independent. Their ability to participate in self-care tasks, like getting dressed, improves.

With more developed vocabulary, they will have greater ability to express feelings through words, rather than behavior (but behaviors still play a large role in toddler emotional expression). Attention spans can vary significantly at this stage, depending on many factors. They may be less likely than their two-year-old self to run from one thing to the next, and more able to stay focused on one game, story, or activity for longer (especially with more practice and exposure to brief, caregiver-led activities that require more focus). Activity needs are still high. Adult supervision can be tapered, depending on the environment and situation. Independence and confidence can strengthen when adults keep a bit of a distance, rather than hovering over their play. Although minor injuries may happen, these are useful opportunities for kids to learn that they can cope with discomfort and also give them more practice with problem-solving and cause and effect.

Ages 4 to 5 Years

There's a reason that formal school begins around age five. This is the time where kids are usually more developmentally ready for the structure and rules of a formal learning environment. They are more independent in daily tasks (though still require supervision and support) and are ready to strengthen relationships outside the family, such as through school, social groups, and playdates.

In terms of communication, children this age are usually able to engage in reciprocal conversations with peers and adults. Emotionally, they may express their feelings verbally, though not necessarily effectively. They may repeat insults or curse words they've heard, or channel their anger toward a loved one with a rousing "I hate you!" Although kids this age can usually cope with some feelings independently, they still benefit from a calming adult presence who can support their emotional expression and regulation.

General Advice for Maintaining Reasonable Expectations

- We all—kids and adults alike—have good and bad days. One tough day or one tough moment does not define you, your child, or your relationship.
- With reasonable expectations, you can meet your child where they are and help them grow into the person they are meant to be.
- Toddlers are always learning and growing. Strengths in some areas and weaknesses in others are normal. Promote learning by leaning on their strengths to support the areas that need more attention.
- Resist any urge to overcompare. Every child is different, and every family is different. Your child's behaviors may look very different from that of your same-age neighbor, or the influencer family you see on social media. There is a wide range of normal development. Consult with your pediatrician if you have concerns about your child's needs.

Learn to Influence Young Children's Behavior

We know toddlers do well when they have predictability and routines in their day, and although they may push back, the more consistency they experience, the easier it is for parents to be proactive in influencing behavior. It's much easier to help kids learn and respond to limits when they are well regulated. Here are some helpful strategies:

- **Use humor and play.** Kids learn best through play. Use playful songs or rhymes to describe what you're doing or what needs to be done. Create games to get through tricky routines in the day, like playfully racing to see who can put on their socks faster. Model the task using beloved toys. Silliness can often help diffuse tension, too.
- **Praise positive behaviors.** Encourage the behavior you want to see more of by calling it out when you see it ("Great job being flexible!" "Thank you for listening!" "I love how you gave your sister a turn with the toy!").
- **Establish routines and talk about plans.** Since kids thrive on predictability, parents can proactively influence children's behaviors by sticking to routines and discussing plans in advance. Although some kids have an easier time going with the flow, you can manage your toddler's expectations by talking about changes in routines or any special plans beforehand.
- **Offer developmentally appropriate explanations for limits.** When kids understand why they are being told to change their behavior, they're more likely to follow through. For toddlers, short and sweet explanations work best ("That glass breaks easily. Please put it down.").
- **Set rules and consistently enforce limits.** Be as consistent as possible when you establish and enforce rules. Your little one may push back at first, but over time, they will learn to accept your rules and limits, and they will understand that you mean what you say.
- **Find ways to say yes.** Hearing a yes is always more comfortable than hearing a no. Try to pause before automatically saying no.

Ask yourself if it's something you could really say yes to. If your toddler asks you to play while you're tending to the baby, instead of saying, "No, I can't play right now," you can say, "Oh yes! We can play as soon as I finish feeding the baby." Also consider if there is a way to say yes within the limit you are setting. For example, if your child asks, "Can I have another cookie?" but you want to enforce a limit, you can say, "You had your cookie for today. You can choose another cookie tomorrow. Do you want it with lunch or dinner?"

Praise and Rewards

Praise can be a powerful tool for learning. When children are praised immediately for specific behaviors, that live feedback helps them learn what to do and that they can replicate that skill in the future. After your child shares a toy with a sibling or peer, instead of praising them with "Good job!" praise the specific behavior: "Great job taking turns!" Depending on their age, you can add an explanation that emphasizes the positive consequences of their behavior, like "Now we can all have fun playing together."

Praise comes in many forms that can yield different outcomes. In psychologist Carol Dweck's research on growth mindset and resilience, she emphasizes praising strategy and process over outcome. This might look like, "I love how you chose to mix blue and purple together. What a great idea!" instead of "You're an amazing artist."

Parents who are concerned that showering their child with too much praise will either be "spoiling" or taking away from intrinsic motivation can be reassured that positive reinforcement and attention is a key process for shaping and influencing all human behavior. This is true even for adults—try effusively thanking your partner for unloading the dishwasher and see what happens! That being said, you don't need to praise your child for every single thing they do. Praise has more power when it's specific and immediate. For behaviors that need additional attention to change, like helping your child learn to ask for a turn instead of grabbing, the child will benefit from a lot of specific praise to connect their behavior to the situation you're trying to teach. Eventually, as these behaviors become more automatic, you can reduce the frequency of praise for these behaviors.

Praise is also useful for modeling positive social skills. When kids hear you expressing gratitude or highlighting their strengths, they are more likely to show the same care toward others. For example, by seeing you model using praise to express gratitude, like "Thank you for passing the carrots," your child will learn how they can show gratitude toward others.

Some parents also wonder about the relationship between rewards and children's internal motivation. Rewards can be a powerful tool for reinforcing children's behaviors as part of the learning process. While some rewards can be tangible, like stickers, ice cream, or a new toy, they don't have to be. For younger toddlers, immediate verbal, enthusiastic praise and physical affection can be most impactful—toddlers thrive on social connection and approval. Positive consequences in the natural environment also can be very rewarding and can be used to support behavior change; for example, "When you put the Legos in the toy bin, then we can go outside to play."

Some parents are curious about using behavior reward charts to influence behaviors. This strategy tends to be more effective for slightly older children, who have a better concept of earning small tokens (such as a sticker on a chart) while working toward a larger reward (such as five stickers equals an extra story at bedtime). If you choose to enlist a chart like this, consider what larger rewards align with your parenting values, and offer reasonable rewards, keeping the following guidelines in mind:

- **Focus on one or two specific behaviors at a time.** Make sure these "target behaviors" are very clearly defined and positively stated ("Use a safe body. Keep your hands and feet to yourself," instead of "Don't hit" or "Be good").

- **Immediate feedback is most effective.** Make sure to give enthusiastic verbal praise along with whatever token you're using for the chart.
- **Break the goal into reasonable chunks.** Consider how frequently the behavior happens: Is it a mealtime behavior, like staying seated? If so, offer your child multiple opportunities to earn the reward each day, such as for each meal and snack.
- **Set your child up for success.** Remind your toddler of the behavior goal before entering a situation, especially where the problem behavior is more likely to occur, and offer frequent verbal praise as they demonstrate the behavior goal. Once a reward is earned, don't remove it—once a paycheck is earned, you're not giving that money back!

Consequences

There has been so much research demonstrating the powerful effects of behavioral tools in parenting, and yet critics have expressed concerns that behavioral approaches are incompatible with connection, neglect a child's internal experience, or liken raising children to training animals. The reality is that authoritative parenting offers space to connect to your child's internal experience while also responding to behaviors with firm limits that teach them about the world.

Our society is designed to provide us with consequences: If you run a red light, you might get a ticket, even if you ran the light because you were distracted by hunger or stress. To raise children to become responsible members of society, parents can help shape their behavior by using consequences. Whenever possible, frame the use of consequences and behavioral corrections as teaching opportunities; this way, you help your toddler learn new skills.

Tips for using consequences with toddlers:

- **Start with proactive tools.** The more positive attention, preparation, and age-appropriate explanations you can provide along the way, the fewer consequences you will need to implement.
- **Use logical, related consequences.** Consequences are most effective as a teaching tool when they relate to the problem. If your toddler is throwing toys, a logical consequence is to remove the toy until the child is ready to play safely. If, instead, when your toddler throws a toy, you tell them, "No dessert tonight!" by the time dessert rolls around, the consequence is much less meaningful. Your toddler probably has forgotten about throwing toys, and the absence of dessert doesn't teach them to play differently in the future.
- **Set the expectation.** In a tricky or unfamiliar environment, tell your child what the behavior expectations are, including what the positive consequence will be if they follow the expectation, and what will happen if they don't. For example, at the start of playground time, you might tell your child, "Stay in the fence, and keep hands and feet to yourself. If you follow the rules, you can keep playing. If you don't follow the rules, we'll have to leave."
- **Highlight positive consequences.** Notice when your child is following the expectation and draw their attention to it with a compliment, such as "Great job keeping your body to yourself! Now we can keep playing."
- **Plan consequences in advance.** Thoughtful consequences that you develop at neutral times protect you from impulsive threats that you might can't follow through on or might later regret, like "If you keep throwing your food, I will cancel your birthday!"
- **Avoid surprises.** Use warnings to make children aware of the consequences before implementing them. Provide brief explanations. "Throwing toys hurts. If you keep throwing toys, you will need to take a break from playing." If and when you need to deliver the

consequence, use a calm, neutral tone to remind them, "You threw the toy. That's not safe, so you need to take a break."

- **Be consistent and follow through.** If you say you're going to leave the park if your toddler hits other kids, you need to be ready and willing to actually leave the park if they continue hitting. Even though they'll likely push back on the consequence, they'll also learn that you mean what you say (see "Prepare for Pushback," page 73).
- **Notice how you feel when delivering consequences.** If you have guilt or hesitation, remind yourself that consequences are part of learning, and you're helping your child learn and grow, which is an expression of love.
- **Use physical intervention, when necessary.** You may need to physically intervene to redirect your child to keep them (or others) safe.

Correcting a Child's Behavior

Much of toddler behavior is driven by exploring curiosities and testing limits. As a result, parents often confront toddler behaviors that need to be corrected or changed because the behaviors are inappropriate, unsafe, or, frankly, just annoying. Depending on the level of severity of the behaviors, here are some ways you can respond to help change or correct your toddler's behaviors:

- **Underreact.** If the behavior is mostly just annoying but not causing any harm, underreaction is your friend. This response is most effective when your toddler's emotions are regulated. Maybe your toddler is dropping their fork from the table and looking expectantly toward you for a reaction. You can first offer a simple verbal correction, like "Forks are for plates or mouths," while replacing the fork on the child's plate. If the behavior continues, gently reduce or remove your attention by removing the object and turning your head or body away briefly. Then redirect your toddler's attention to something else, where you can re-engage with them enthusiastically, such as saying, "Ooh, your potatoes look good! Did you try them yet?" Toddlers will learn that those minor misbehaviors don't get a big reaction out of you, so they will be less likely to continue, and they will be more likely to seek out interactions that elicit positive attention and engagement.

- **Enlist selective attention.** Behaviors can be influenced by parents' selective attention. Ignore or underreact to behaviors that you want to decrease, while simultaneously looking out for desirable behaviors that you can give attention to. For example, during a meltdown, if your toddler takes a deep breath in the midst of kicking and screaming, give attention to the calming skill, such as "Nice deep breath. That helps," while removing attention from the kicking and screaming (as long as everyone is physically safe).
- **Explain.** Offer a brief and simple explanation for why the behavior is being corrected.
- **Model and redirect to an appropriate alternative behavior.** Tell your child what to do, instead of what not to do. Instead of "Don't draw on the walls," gently redirect your child to an appropriate space for their artistic expression: "Crayons are for paper. Here's some paper you can use." You can also use logical consequences here, as discussed above, like involving your toddler in cleaning the crayon marks off the wall.
- **Co-regulate first.** If a behavior correction leads to a tantrum, start by helping your child regulate (see "How to Soothe and Support," page 87), and then guide them to follow through with the corrective behavior. Once regulated, they may be able to complete the task independently, or they may need your help. For example, if your child throws toys when it's time to clean up, start by helping

them regulate their emotional response to cleanup time, then meet them at their level to help them follow through on putting the toys in the bin gently.

- **Provide a timeout.** When used sparingly alongside positive, proactive parenting strategies, timeout can be an effective tool for addressing highly aggressive or otherwise problematic behaviors. Although some people worry that timeout may be overly harsh or may harm a child's attachment relationship, research shows that timeout is a useful tool that actually supports a strong parent-child attachment and is in line with authoritative parenting when used appropriately. Timeouts can be helpful for reducing child behavior problems and giving parents and children a moment to self-regulate. Modeling a calm demeanor can help maintain connection and attachment security while holding the boundary. The message throughout timeout communicates that the child is loved and cared for, and that the timeout is a response to a specific behavior. Some parents use the reframe of a "time-in," where they remove their child from the challenging environment, coach their child to cope through their big feelings, and then when regulated, help their child correct the behavior. See page 70 for more details about how to implement a timeout.

While some kids may readily accept corrective feedback, others may have a negative reaction to being corrected. They may feel ashamed or sad by the correction, or angry that they can't do what they wanted to do. Connect with your child by coming in close at eye level, offering physical affection, and acknowledging how you think they may be feeling: "I know you are disappointed that you have to take a break from playing. When you can use safe hands, we can play together again."

Also, no matter how frustrating the problem behavior is to you as a parent, once a behavior has been corrected or the consequence has been provided, do your best to move forward. Let go of grudges, and

How to Give a Timeout as an Authoritative Parent

1. **Plan and practice.** Introduce the timeout plan during a calm moment, and practice the following steps. You can practice by using a toy or stuffed animal to show your child what to expect. Name the behaviors that will result in a timeout, including any nonnegotiable family rules (like hitting a sibling) and any time you give a warning, as described below. Identify a place where timeout will occur that is free from distractions and where you can still keep an eye on them, like a designated chair. Make sure to give lots of praise for your child's involvement in practicing!

2. **Warning.** When your child does something that warrants a timeout according to the expectations you set, start by providing a simple, matter-of-fact warning using a calm tone. For example, your child dumps out a bin of Magna-Tiles and scatters them around the floor. If after telling them to "Please put the Magna-Tiles back in the bin," they seem to ignore you, give a clear warning to remind them of the consequence for not listening: "If you don't put your Magna-Tiles in the bin, you will need to go to the timeout chair." If after the warning, your child starts doing what you told them to do, then awesome job! Give them some enthusiastic praise, like "Thank you so much for listening!"

3. **Timeout time.** If after the warning, and about five seconds of waiting (count in your head to allow your child time to process and respond), your child still doesn't do what you told them to do, name the consequence with a simple statement: "You didn't do what I told you to do, so you need to sit in the timeout chair." Immediately take your child to the timeout chair, and tell them to stay there until you say it's time to get off. Timeout can last about three minutes—this is enough time away from the reinforcing environment to communicate that the behavior is not acceptable.

4. **Corrective action.** At the end of three minutes, ask your child if they are ready to reengage with the initial task or appropriate behavior. For example: "Are you ready to come back and put the Magna-Tiles in the bin?" or, in the case of aggressive behavior, "Are you ready to come back and play safely?" Then guide your child to follow through with the corrective action.

5. **End with positivity and enthusiasm.** Offer enthusiastic praise for your child engaging in the appropriate behavior. Although you may have felt frustrated at points throughout the process, try to move forward knowing that you have provided a consistent, predictable consequence that will help shape your child's future, and jump right back in to using your positive, playful parenting skills that elevate joy between you and your child.

Remember, timeout is most useful when used consistently, though sparingly, as a consequence for predetermined behaviors. Start with positive and proactive strategies first!

don't introduce a new consequence hours later, long after they've forgotten what happened. Take a breather if you need (and compliment yourself for your skillful work in helping your child learn new skills and accepting their feelings), and then try to reset with your child by incorporating the PRIDE skills from page 55, reconnecting through positive interactions.

WHAT'S OFF THE TABLE, AND WHY

Once you're armed with the proactive strategies to influence toddler behavior, a large dose of positive attention and connection throughout each day, and the smaller, necessary dose of behavioral corrections and consequences that will surely come up, you'll be well on your way to achieving your authoritative parenting goals. On the flip side, let's explore some parenting behaviors that are considered "off the table"—either because they are explicitly harmful or they are not known to be particularly helpful.

- **Spanking and physical punishment.** Although physical punishment may stop a child's problematic behavior in the immediate moment, physical punishment communicates to children that they are not physically safe with the adults they thought they could trust. It also instills a sense of fear that has long-standing negative impacts on development, and models to children that problems can be solved by hurting others. Parents who might feel an urge to spank or physically punish their children should first recognize this urge, take a moment to self-regulate (see "Self-Soothe and Self-Regulate," page 85), then use one of the other strategies to correct or influence your child's behavior.
- **Inappropriate use of timeouts.** Timeouts aren't appropriate for behaviors beyond a child's control, such as when they spill something or can't complete a task. Timeout is also not appropriate for attachment-related behaviors, like expressions of fear or distress.

Additionally, isolating toddlers for more than a few minutes can increase distress and confuse the child in the moment.

- **Threatening to leave.** It can be tempting, but threatening to leave your child (even though you don't mean it) can be a significant rupture to your toddler's sense of safety and trust in you as their loving, protective caregiver.
- **Criticism and shaming.** Excessive shaming, especially when it suggests a criticism of the child's character, is harmful to a child's self-esteem and ruptures their connection with you. Focus the feedback on correcting the problematic behavior, rather than criticizing the character of the child.

Prepare for Pushback

When we make a change in how we set a limit or respond to our children's difficult behaviors, we can expect that those behaviors will get worse before they get better. After all, kids are meant to test limits. Pushback does not mean you're doing the wrong thing. It means your child is learning, and ultimately, they will find comfort and security in the "bigger, stronger, wiser" person keeping them safe.

When behaviors intensify in response to a boundary or limit, this is called an **extinction burst**. Imagine a scenario where every time your child whines for an extra cookie at dessert, you give them an extra cookie. Eventually, you decide to set a new boundary and not give in to your child's whining. The first time you do this, aren't they going to whine more than they ever have before? From their perspective, whining got them what they wanted in the past, so why won't it now? Maybe if they just whine a bit louder and longer, you'll give the cookie. And you can't stand the escalation in whining! So . . . okay, fine, you give the cookie. You'll try again tomorrow. And the cycle continues. Your child learns that they just need to raise the intensity of the whining to get the cookie.

How to Set Your Boundary

- Prepare your child in advance. Using simple language, explain the new boundary to your child—preferably well before you set it. Explain what you plan to do. For example, if you're setting a boundary about playing safely to prevent aggressive behaviors:
    - Explain the rationale: "Playtime is fun when we use a calm body and safe hands."
    - Explain the expectation: "When you're playing with your brother, play with gentle hands."
    - Help your child practice following the boundary: "Playing gently looks like this."
    - Explain the consequences, including what will happen if they both break and follow the rule: "If you hit, you will take a break from playing," and if they follow the rule: "If you play gently, I'm going to say 'Hooray!' and you can keep playing and having fun."
- Remind your child of the rules and boundaries when you enter situations where those limits might be tested.
- Offer a lot of behavior-specific praise to any positive responses they make to the boundary, such as effort to respect a boundary.

How to Maintain Your Boundary

- Notice what thoughts and feelings come up for you when boundaries are tested. Is it shame, self-doubt, fear of judgment by observers?

- Take a few regulating deep breaths.
- Remind yourself that kids are meant to test limits. This is part of learning. Holding boundaries, despite protests, communicates to children that you are a strong and wise adult who will keep them safe.
- Remember that with consistency, pushback won't last forever. Kids will learn to tolerate the boundaries and rules when they see they are firm.
- Expect an extinction burst and plan ahead for how you will ride it out—deep breaths, positive self-talk, a reminder that boundary testing is learning.
- Tell your child what options are available within the boundary, redirecting attention away from what is not available. For example, when maintaining a boundary around limiting screentime to one episode of *Paw Patrol*, redirect your child's attention to what they can play with when TV time is over, or when they may be able to watch *Paw Patrol* next.
- Prepare for the possibility of physical intervention in order to hold a boundary. When an impulsive three-year-old swings their arm back ready to take a hit at their sister, parents can gently but firmly grab the toddler's arm to keep them from hitting and say, "No hitting" or "We don't hit."

Negotiations and Power Struggles

In a toddler's seemingly unending efforts to exert autonomy and control, their pushback on a parental limit may turn into a power struggle. As much as we may wish, we cannot entirely control our children's behaviors; we can only control aspects of the environment and our own actions in an effort to influence their behaviors. By utilizing the parenting tools we've discussed, parents are likely to experience fewer power struggles. However, if and when you do find yourself in a negotiation match with your toddler, enlist the following strategies:

- When you find yourself in a power struggle with a toddler who seems to always say no:
    - Only emphasize essential boundaries. Selectively choose the demands you are placing on your child—the more demands they receive, the harder it will be to meet every one.
    - Validate their feelings or perspective.
    - Offer simple rationales for why a rule or expectation is being set.
    - Offer choices when possible within the limits.
    - Recognize when the back-and-forth of negotiations ("But I want to go to the playground!") is giving too much power to their pushback (which reinforces the behavior), and end the interaction. Expect that extinction burst—the screaming, crying, name-calling—and do your best to ride it out without giving more direct attention to the interaction. As soon as your child starts to calm down and engage appropriately, give a lot of positive attention and praise for their appropriate behavior, including their readiness to solve the problem calmly.
    - Catch your child being flexible. When your child who almost always says no is able to go with the flow or be flexible, offer enthusiastic praise for how flexible they're being. More positive attention toward flexibility will help them to be more flexible in the future.
- When you find yourself negotiating with a child who expresses a strong preference for one parent or caregiver over another:

- Prepare your child in advance.
    - Explain the rationale: "Nana and I both love you a lot. We both love taking care of you, and we both have other jobs at home, too."
    - Explain the expectation: "Some nights, Nana will read and put you to bed, and some nights, I will read and put you to bed. But we will both kiss you good night."
- Help your child practice following the boundary: "You might feel disappointed if Nana is not your first choice. When you miss me, you can give your blankie an extra cuddle, or look at the picture of you and me together. Remember, you will see me in the morning."
- Offer a lot of behavior-specific praise to how they respond to the boundary: "You did a great job reading with Nana last night!"

- When you feel like you're constantly battling with a child who's refusing to try new things:
    - Don't go all-in to force your child to try something new. Recognize that their refusal may be their effort to communicate their own boundaries, whether due to a sense of insecurity, danger, or anxiety. What may look like obstinance for the sake of obstinance might be your child's effort to communicate a problem. Consider the "why" behind the behavior (see "Decoding Difficult Behaviors," page 33).
    - Catch your child being brave trying something new. Focus positive attention toward bravery and flexibility!

- Break the new thing into smaller, more manageable chunks, and encourage your child to try a small component or to approach the experience together. With warmth and compassion, you can provide the hands-on support they may need to try something new.

Chapter 3

Surviving Tears, Tantrums, and Triggers

This chapter will provide an overview of emotion regulation in children and adults, to offer parents a deeper understanding of the role emotions play in parent-child interactions and child behaviors. I hope you gain from this chapter a greater awareness around your own emotions, as well as your toddler's. With this insight into how emotions work and the role they play, you'll be even more equipped to use these practical tools to help tolerate and tame children's crying and meltdowns—as well as your own emotions that come up in response.

The Deal with Dysregulation

Emotions are a normative and healthy part of the human experience. In fact, emotions are some of the first and most primitive responses that infants experience. Sure, emotions develop complexity over time, but intense emotional responses are necessary and adaptive right from birth. Child development experts Daniel Siegel and Tina Payne Bryson describe a child's developing brain in several parts. The bottom floor, or the "downstairs brain," contains the most primitive part of our brain, responsible for basic functions and strong emotions. Typically well developed from birth, the downstairs brain operates automatically, instinctively, and, at times, reactively. Drs. Siegel and Bryson note that in young kids, the "upstairs brain"—which controls more complex thinking, rationalizing, problem-solving, and perspective taking—is under construction.

In infants, emotional expression looks like crying when hungry, tired, uncomfortable, or in need of a cuddle. In toddlers, this might look like crying, screaming, or throwing materials (or themselves) on the floor. This is all normal, since their ability to regulate these processes is under construction. Ultimately, most parents would love to see their children easily cope with their emotions, perhaps by politely and calmly saying, "I'm disappointed that we have to leave the park. But I understand that we have to go pick up my brother from school, so I will come straight to the car." Wouldn't that be nice? Just calm words and no tears? But, of course, this is not even close to how toddlers operate.

Most parents find it challenging to know how to respond to toddlers' emotions—how much crying to tolerate, what to do when the crying doesn't seem to end, or when the tantrum spirals into aggressive behaviors. Emotions are normal and allowed, though not every behavioral expression of emotions is acceptable. Sometimes emotional expression rises to a level of frequency, intensity, and difficulty to manage that interferes with other tasks or routines in a way that is more pervasively problematic, which we might refer to as emotion **dysregulation**. Dysregulation is the state of being out of control, unable to manage emotions.

Dysregulation in Adults

It is *very* normal for your toddler to evoke an emotional response in you—whether you're reacting to the feelings of joy and pride in seeing them climb to a new height on the jungle gym, or feelings of frustration after your 10th time telling them to put away their toys. It's also very normal for your patience as a parent to be tested.

When regulated, our upstairs and downstairs brains work together. However, there are times when the automatic, intense emotional response of the downstairs brain gets activated, overriding the upstairs brain's ability to rationalize, problem-solve, and slow us down. Sometimes, this is adaptive—it's helpful for our downstairs brains to fully take over with an automatic response when there's a real threat in the environment. When you step into the street and a car horn blares, your downstairs brain takes over to help you jump back onto the curb without thinking twice. But sometimes, the downstairs brain takes over when there's a false alarm—a perception of a true threat in the environment when really the environment is safe.

This can happen when you're triggered by your toddler's emotions or behaviors (see "What to Do When You're Triggered," page 84), when your skillful-parent battery has been depleted from a draining day with your kids or chronic stress at work or in your personal life, or when you have a physiological need, like feeling exhausted or hungry. Adults who are generally more prone to anxiety, have difficulties regulating their mood, or have a history of trauma may also have a lower threshold for feeling dysregulated.

When your downstairs brain is in overdrive, you might be more likely to lose your temper or revert to some reactive parenting responses, perhaps ones that you witnessed as a child from your own caregivers. In these moments, the most powerful first step to waking up your upstairs brain is simply to bring your awareness to the experience. Using a simple statement to label your emotion, like "I'm feeling overwhelmed/frustrated/angry/stressed," helps reengage your upstairs brain by verbalizing what is otherwise an intense, automatic experience. Taking slow, deep breaths can also help start the physiological reset your body needs.

Dysregulation in Young Children

Because a young child's upstairs brain is still under construction, we *expect* them to act irrationally and fall apart when faced with a big emotion. When this happens, consider it an opportunity to help your child learn to understand and cope with their feelings. While there are certain aspects of brain development that come with time, the more you can help your child work through big feelings, the better equipped they'll be to navigate emotions throughout their life. All children will face challenges and stressors throughout their lifetime. Although at times we wish we could just change the circumstance that is causing the big emotion, that's not always realistic or productive; in fact, teaching them to recognize feelings and cope with challenges from an early age is a tremendous gift.

When kids don't have the words to express their thoughts and feelings verbally (and even sometimes when they do!), they will show us how they're feeling through their actions. Behavior is communication. Big emotions that lead to meltdowns can occur in response to anything from separating from a beloved caregiver to being presented with their apple cut into slices instead of whole (even though they first told you they wanted it cut, and maybe they even melted down yesterday when you gave them a whole apple).

From Co-Regulation to Self-Regulation

Kids learn through the context of their relationships. Consider how you might teach your child to put on shoes. At first, you put on their shoes for them. Then you might help them put on their shoes; perhaps by opening the shoe and encouraging them to slide their foot in, and maybe tapping on their foot if they need another physical cue. Gradually, you reduce your support and involvement until your child can put shoes on independently. This gradual process of reducing hands-on support is called **scaffolding**. Learning to regulate emotions works similarly. Kids learn how to respond to and express their own emotions by the modeling they see from their parents' emotional expression—both in terms of how parents respond to their own emotions and how they coach kids to process theirs.

Self-regulation is the ability to modulate emotions independently, which might even include a child recognizing the need to seek support from a trusted adult. To help children develop skills in self-regulation, it's always good to remember to manage your expectations for your child's skills based on their age and developmental level. It's also helpful to remember that a child's ability to regulate emotions independently might vary depending on the environment (such as at daycare versus home, or with a parent versus a grandparent), as well as on physiological factors (are they hungry? Tired? Overstimulated?).

To teach self-regulation, you'll want to begin from a place of **co-regulation**. Co-regulation is when a trusted adult responsively connects with the child to regulate together (whether or not the adult is dysregulated in the moment, too, like when tensions are high). As you join with your child to regulate emotional responses, you can use the tools in this chapter for both yourself and your child. Consider how you're modeling your use of calming skills in other contexts (and even with other dysregulated responses to emotions, such as yelling, storming off, shutting down, or slamming doors).

For some children, learning to regulate emotions does not necessarily take a normative developmental path. If your child continues to prove difficult to soothe after consistent efforts to implement some of the strategies in this chapter, it's worth consulting with your pediatrician to rule out other potential developmental factors that may be contributing, such as developmental delays, language disorders, autism or sensory processing difficulties, or ADHD.

What to Do When You're Triggered

All parents lose patience with their kids at times. What causes you to pop might be different from what sets off your partner or friend. When triggered, your fight-flight-freeze high-alert system is activated, reacting as if there is a danger in the environment. Try to pay attention to physical signs in your body, like an increased heart rate or body temperature, sweaty palms, or muscle tension. These physical signs are a clue to reset before reengaging. Our goal here as parents isn't to avoid all triggers. More realistically and importantly, we can build an awareness of what pushes our buttons and plan ahead for how to cope.

Learn Your Triggers

As parents, we're not only triggered simply by the fact that our toddler pinched us for the third time today—sometimes there's more going on within us. Common triggers for parents may be physiological: lack of sleep or exercise, hunger, sensitivity to noise, too much caffeine. Other triggers that may or may not happen in the scope of parenting include sensitive beliefs about ourselves, like feeling misunderstood or disrespected, feeling excluded, or worrying that someone may be mad at us. Others may be related to an interference with our values, like feeling rushed or experiencing a lack of control when we prioritize being organized. When triggered, we might notice muscle tension; irritability; feelings of shutting down or overstimulation; or an urge to yell or physically exert control, snap at others, or withdraw/disconnect by leaving the room, zoning out, or reaching for our phones to mindlessly scroll.

Self-Soothe and Self-Regulate

Despite your best efforts to equip yourself with proactive parenting tools, if you're triggered by your toddler during their meltdown, you might struggle to access your skillful parent toolkit. This is understandable, and here's my advice: Once you've identified that you're feeling triggered, pause to regulate yourself so you can more skillfully attend to your child. All you need to make sure of is that your child is in a physically safe space before you step away, even if it means physically putting them in their crib despite protests, so you can take the moment you need to reset.

From here:

- **Attend to your physical needs.** Start by taking a few calming breaths. If your reaction is triggered by hunger, eat; if triggered by a lack of physical activity all day, give yourself a minute to jog in place. Proactively, if you know that getting your toddler through their bedtime routine is always a challenge because you don't get a moment's rest all day, take a few minutes to give yourself what you need, whether that's a nutritious snack, a cup of tea, or a moment to breathe before starting.

- **Find a change of scene.** Stepping away from a triggering environment can help your body reset and experience a sense of safety. Step into another room, or step outside to take a few deep breaths of fresh air.

- **Change your body temperature.** A very cold drink of water or wet washcloth on your neck can quickly cool your dysregulated nervous system.
- **Reduce intensity of sensations.** If noise is triggering, take a break in a quieter space, put in ear plugs, or turn on calming music. If it's bright lights or a smell, combat the reaction with a contrasting sensation (for example, smell something pleasant, dim the lights, or take a break in a dark room).
- **Move your body.** Channel the body's natural urge to fight or run away into movement. Jump, shake, dance it out, do a few push-ups. A quick physical activity will help release that energy.
- **Seek social support.** Call a friend or partner who can validate, encourage, and empathize with you.
- **Seek physical comfort.** A tight hug with a partner or a cuddle with a pet can aid in soothing yourself.
- **Name the feeling.** Verbalizing how you feel to yourself or a friend will help reinforce your awareness and aid the process of emotion regulation. Say it using an "I feel" statement, like "I feel overwhelmed" or "I feel frustrated." "I feel" statements offer distance between you and the feeling, while also reminding us that the feeling is a temporary state.
- **Repeat positive self-talk or a supportive mantra.** What advice would you give a good friend? Maybe it's a reminder that this moment will pass; things won't be hard forever. Just a reminder that you can cope and will get to the other side, or that your child's only two, and this is what two-year-olds do. You are a strong, capable parent. One interaction does not define you, your child, or your relationship.
- **Call for backup.** Sometimes, your toddler's tantrum may be too big or may feel too overwhelming that the above reset strategies just

aren't enough. Although it's not always feasible, if there is another caregiver available, swap out. This gives you a much-needed break, while also giving your toddler a reset from another supportive caregiver.

How to Soothe and Support

There are many ways to respond to your child's big emotions while still holding a boundary. Let's face it, an inconsolable tantrum after turning off the TV or trying to leave the park is not an indication that our child needs to watch more TV or stay at the park 10 minutes longer. We can validate their emotional experience while helping them calm down *and* hold the boundary. This is actually the crux of authoritative parenting: pairing responsiveness and warmth with firm limits. Build your confidence by reminding yourself how helpful it is to teach kids how to tolerate disappointment. The tips offered here can be used together or on their own, in any order that's helpful for you:

- **Proactively, teach through daily modeling.** You can build your family's language around emotions through everyday activities. When familiar skills and tools are integrated into daily routines, it's much easier for children to access those skills in the throes of a tantrum. Label your and your child's emotions throughout the day and talk about how you will cope. Here are two examples, which you can adapt around your child's language and developmental levels:
    - Model expressing disappointment and being flexible by saying something like, "Oh no! I wanted a banana but we don't have any. I'm feeling disappointed. I'll have an apple instead. I'll add bananas to our grocery list for tomorrow."

- Model taking a deep breath to soothe anger: "I'm feeling mad that I spilled coffee on the floor! I'll take a deep breath [pause to demonstrate]. Now I feel calmer, so I can clean up."

- **Get close.** When big emotions overwhelm your child, calmly and slowly move your body physically closer to your child's and get on their level. This communicates your supportive presence. While physically close, label the emotion you see your child expressing.
- **Physically assist.** Sometimes toddler emotions are triggered by their difficulty completing a task. If your child is frustrated because they can't open their water bottle, help them open the bottle while acknowledging their frustration.
- **Label and validate emotions.** Label the emotions you observe your child expressing. Let them know it's okay to feel that way and you understand (even if the reaction seems totally irrational to your adult brain—you can express compassion and understanding without necessarily agreeing!).
- **Share deep breaths.** Taking deep, calming breaths is a powerful way to soothe a dysregulated nervous system. Parents can help soothe their children by modeling and joining them in a deep breath together. This can be done by showing them what to do, or by simply breathing together, deeply and wordlessly, while embraced in a hug. Just like infants are soothed by the deep breaths when nuzzled onto a parent's chest, many toddlers find this intimate co-regulation technique calming, too, as they match the slower-paced breaths that parents model.
- **Use imagery.** Kids benefit from visual imagery to use with calming skills. Although prompting a deep breath alone might be enough for some kids, others benefit from a cue to imagine breathing deeply. For example, encourage your child to inhale through their nose to pretend to smell the flowers, and exhale through their mouth as if blowing out a birthday candle (or inhaling to "smell" a

favorite food, and exhaling through the mouth to "cool it down"). You can also help your toddler imagine a calming place by describing imagery associated with their happy place.

- **Use body sensations.** Other body-calming techniques can be soothing for co-regulation, such as rubbing your child's back or telling a calming story while drawing a picture with your finger on their back. You can also encourage your child to release some of the dysregulated energy by pretending to squeeze a lemon as hard as they can in their fists to make lemonade, or engaging more actively through jumping or dancing.
- **Engage with the five senses.** Help soothe your child by grounding them in the present using their five senses. Focus attention on the sights, sounds, scents, textures, and tastes in their immediate surroundings. Some kids can even be soothed by focusing on just one sense; for example, encourage your child to look for something red, orange, yellow, etc.
- **Reduce stimulation.** Sometimes co-regulation requires removing excess stimulation or changing the environment, such as dimming lights, moving into a smaller or quieter space, turning off noisy toys, or playing calming music. Stepping outside to get a burst of fresh air or taking a bath can also help the body physiologically reset.
- **Redirect.** After decreasing the emotional intensity, you can redirect your child's attention. Toddlers often need help moving forward from a setback so they won't ruminate on negative emotions and experiences for too long. You can also use humor and distraction to defuse tension when your little one expresses intense emotions; for example, by redirecting them to play a silly face game or telling a favorite story.
- **Provide a calming corner.** It can be helpful to create a calm space in your home where kids can go to calm down. A calming corner

might have cozy pillows, dim lighting, books, a music player, and some drawing materials. When emotions start rising, encourage or bring your child to self-soothe in their calming corner to prevent them from getting too dysregulated.

- **Be the voice of calm even when they're not.** Your child may be so upset that they yell "Go away!" Maintain a calm demeanor, and avoid getting too focused on their dysregulated tone. As long as your child is physically safe, you can offer space and calmly remind them that you're available when they need you. You might say, "I understand you want to be alone. I'll be right over here when you're ready." Keep a close eye out so you can step in when they're ready for you, and consider checking in periodically to offer additional soothing support.

Whether you're juggling multiple kids' needs or you're in a rush to get somewhere, realistically, parents may not be able to give their full attention to each toddler emotional outburst every single time. This is completely understandable. If you can channel even one of these tips to begin working through a tough moment, you'll be working toward helping your child regulate. There may be times when you don't have the time or energy to ride the whole wave of emotions with them. In these cases, you might need to physically intervene, whether to keep them safe or to move on with your day. If your child is refusing to put on pants and you need to leave the house, do your best to continue modeling calm composure and labeling their experience while also firmly putting their pants on and swooping them out the door.

Notice the Early Signs

Anyone who has spent a day with a toddler knows that their emotions can escalate from 0 to 60 in a second, seemingly without warning. Sometimes we can identify the reason for the eruption, like transitioning to a less-preferred activity. Other times, toddlers' emotions can seem completely mysterious. Generally, we can mitigate the intensity of big emotions by being proactive, such as by preparing kids for transitions, planning ahead for tricky environments, and being mindful of their moodiest times of day. Toddlers are especially prone to tantrums when tired, hungry, frustrated, or in need of attention, so it can help to be mindful of whether your toddler's basic needs have been met. On days when they refuse a nap or after a rough night of sleep, give yourself some grace and acknowledge that everyone's fuse might be a bit shorter. Bring snacks and favorite toys on outings to make sure your toddler is nourished and has comforting options for play.

Your toddler may give you some early physical signs that a big emotion might be brewing, maybe by vocalizing frustration (words or sounds), clenching fists, tightening other muscles, or even exhibiting excessive silliness. In these moments, try to offer brief support to calmly help your child through the difficult situation and redirect their attention and energy.

Ride the Wave with Them

When kids are flooded with intense emotions, before helping problem-solve or correct a behavior, we need to help them cope, or "ride the wave" of the big emotion. Through co-regulation, parents can help kids learn to cope with their big feelings. Often, this co-regulation is mutually beneficial, as parents may start to feel their emotions rising, too.

1. Start by soothing yourself. A deep breath, a pep talk, whatever you need to quickly fill your tank to be ready to ride the wave with your toddler.

2. Validate and label the child's feelings. If you're not sure, guess or describe what you see.

3. Try a calming strategy or two (see "How to Soothe and Support," page 87) with them, like deep breathing.

4. Help them solve the problem, if necessary.
5. Redirect your child's attention to something else. Once you've acknowledged the feeling and helped them cope, you can support a shift in their attention.

Support the Inconsolable

All kids have different levels of sensitivity. Some are more flexible and quick to adapt and soothe, whereas other kids may experience emotions more intensely. Emotions are very physical experiences, and for some kids, when that emotional downstairs brain takes over, the physical sensations they feel in their body may be highly uncomfortable and overwhelming.

It might take some trial and error to find what works for your little one, depending on the situation. Some kids benefit from a tight hug and physical closeness to regulate, while other kids need more physical space. For these kids, parents can communicate their physical presence as they sit nearby and calmly say, "I'm here" while continuing to use soothing skills themselves, serving as a model for their dysregulated toddler. No matter how your child soothes, praise their efforts toward calm, saying things like, "Nice deep breath. That seems to help you feel calmer." And in those times when it feels like they might never stop crying, hang in there. They eventually will. You've got this.

Talk and Check in Later

Kids have an easier time learning to self-regulate when they have opportunities to practice when they are calm.

- When reading books or watching TV, parents can help kids talk about the characters' emotions. Observe how certain situations bring up different feelings for different people.

- Talk about your own emotions and how you cope. Use examples in your daily life to increase your family's emotion vocabulary. "I couldn't find my keys. I was frustrated, but I took deep breaths to calm down. I found them on the chair!"
- Depending on their age, developmental stage, and language skills, your child may be able to process a previous meltdown with you at a later time, when everyone is calmer. Together, you can tell the story about what happened, how each person felt, what helped, what didn't help, and what would be helpful in the future. Some kids might feel shame about the experience and may have a hard time talking about it. Don't force it. You can tell a similar story about a friend or character, as it can be easier for kids to talk about someone else's experience rather than their own.

What NOT to Do

When toddlers are having a tantrum, dysregulated, or recovering from a meltdown, they're not able to take in much of what parents want to say. Even so, it can be hard for many parents to resist the urge to try to teach their kid a lesson in that moment. Here are some common missteps to avoid when trying to correct or address toddler behaviors and emotions—they are often ineffective and can be counterproductive.

- **Ask very young kids to "use their words."** Some toddlers may not have the words to express themselves in that moment. And even those who do have the expressive language skills won't be able to access their skillful language when dysregulated. When parents want to model and teach appropriate language use—such as "using words" instead of whining—it's much more helpful to model and guide your child with what specifically to say instead. Start by guiding them to take a calming breath and tell them, using developmentally appropriate language in your calm adult voice, what to say instead ("You're so frustrated that you can't open that package! You can say, 'Grandma, help please.'" And "Great job using kind words to ask for help").

- **Shame and blame.** All feelings are okay, even when the behavior used to communicate the feelings might not be. Shaming or blaming kids invalidates their feelings, and can rupture your connection by communicating that you can't handle their feelings (all the more distressing when kids are feeling out of control and seeking a wiser caregiver to help them feel contained). Instead, name the feeling you observe and try to soothe. Notice if your urge to shame or blame is because your triggers are activated (see "What to Do When You're Triggered," page 84).
- **Rationalize and overexplain.** In the midst of a meltdown, less is more. Offering a lengthy explanation or trying to justify a situation may be too much information. When you need to remove your child from a situation during a meltdown, simply say, "I'm doing this to keep you safe" in a calm tone to avoid too much power struggle and confusion.
- **Ask too many questions.** When kids are dysregulated, questions can feel overwhelming and insurmountable. Instead, try describing what you're observing, in brief, simple language while offering comfort. Instead of "What happened?" try, "You're crying. Ouch, that hurt when you fell. Poppy's here."

When You Want to Give In or Change Your Mind

As parents, sometimes we decide that maintaining a boundary isn't worth the tears and pushback, or we don't have the emotional or physical energy to consistently hold a boundary we previously set. This happens, and while children learn best with predictable consistency, you won't cause irreparable damage by making an occasional decision to relax a boundary.

Ideally, if you're going to change your mind about holding a boundary, the best approach is one that doesn't reinforce undesirable behaviors. If your child is screaming and crying for a candy bar at the grocery store checkout line, and you've already said no, eventually giving in and buying that candy bar will communicate to your child that if they escalate their protests to that high intensity in the future, they will get what they want. Using this example, here are a few tips that can help you adjust your boundaries without reinforcing undesirable behaviors.

- **First, try to help your child engage in an alternate, appropriate, calming behavior.** Before buying the candy bar in response to your child's screams and demands, co-regulate by leading them in a calming breath and then prompting them to ask for the candy with calm, kind words. In doing so, you can then enthusiastically praise and reinforce the appropriate request, rather than giving in to the candy solely in response to crying and screaming.

- **Hold part of the boundary.** You might decide to give in to purchasing the candy (hopefully after your child has requested it with calm, kind words), but establish a new boundary around when they may eat the treat. Set the expectation that they will get to eat it for snack time at home, or after lunch. By delaying the reward, you break the cycle of the immediate reinforcement of the checkout-line screams.

- **Recognize the pattern and plan ahead for next time.** If you start to notice more boundary testing in certain situations, these are situations to plan ahead for in the future. If it's an environment (like a grocery store checkout line), or transition time (like leaving the playground or going to bed), you can prepare yourself and your child by setting expectations and planning for these tough moments in advance.

Part 2

Strategies and Suggestions

Now that you've taken a deeper dive into some of the foundational principles of child development, behavior and emotion regulation, and authoritative parenting behaviors, it's time to apply those skills to specific situations. I've provided a collection of ideas and strategies to help you tackle common parenting situations and challenges in a way that aligns with authoritative parenting behaviors. The tips that follow are intended to be accessible to all without requiring excessive time or resources, and they are merely suggestions. You know yourself, your family, and your child best. Take what works for you, and trust yourself.

Chapter 4

General Toddler Needs

All parents experience some challenges and frustrations with basic toddler needs, like eating, sleeping, and toileting. While there are many ways to approach these tasks, we can experience the most success when we support our children with a sense of confidence and competence in our own skills, an acceptance of our own flaws, and the balance of love, warmth, and ability to hold firm boundaries. This chapter offers skills to help build your confidence in handling common toddler needs with an authoritative approach.

- Eating
- Sleeping
- Toileting
- Learning
- Socializing

Eating

A Practical Overview

The transition from baby to toddler around eating can be both exciting and daunting. Many families embrace eating routines, rituals, and recipes that reflect their cultural identities, traditions, and values. Toddlerhood offers another opportunity: for parents to set a foundation for their children's future attitudes and behaviors regarding food.

During the early childhood years, a child's food intake and preferences can vary widely depending on the child and on the stage they're in—a two-year-old might eat fewer foods and less quantity than they did just a few months before. As long as caregivers provide a broad and nourishing range of foods, cumulative food intake over the course of a week is more representative of a child's nourishment than one meal.

Authoritative parents can support the development of their child's autonomy while setting up an environment for success. Authoritative parents also avoid harsh, coercive parenting practices, like pressuring, forcing or bribing children to eat, or restricting certain foods. These types of coercive practices are associated with a poor relationship with food, poor awareness of body fullness and hunger cues, and a lower-quality diet over time.

Eating can be a common area for power struggles, but these can be minimized and overcome when caregivers establish a structure within which children can exert power and choice. Childhood eating specialists emphasize the concept of "division of responsibility" to distinguish parents' and children's roles in eating habits. In this framework, parents' jobs are to establish and maintain structure related to eating habits, including the "when, where, and what" of eating. Kids also have their own responsibilities: Within the structure set by parents, kids' jobs are to decide whether to eat and how much. When toddlers and preschoolers are presented with the agency to choose within their parents' limits, kids develop their autonomy, awareness of internal fullness and hunger cues, and acceptance of their own food preferences (which we all have!).

Child's Perspective and Challenges

A toddler's drive for independence and their interests in exploring and experimenting can create both challenges and opportunities during mealtimes. Some toddlers are excited by the novelty of a new food, whereas others are skeptical. Some kids are sensitive to unfamiliar food textures and flavors and may need to be exposed to foods many times before being ready to try something new or retry a food they previously rejected.

Toddlers may exert their independence and control by expressing food preferences. Toddlers who have less control over their daily environment in general may be more likely to try to exert control through asserting strong preferences and selectivity around their food, and even its presentation, at mealtimes.

As they transition from babies who were entirely dependent on adults to direct their eating, toddlers start to build an awareness of the internal body signals that they are hungry or full. It's important for us to pay attention and respect their signs of both hunger and fullness. Being pressured to eat can confuse kids' abilities to listen to their own body and interfere with the development of self-regulation.

Parent's Perspective and Needs

Although food can be a tremendous source of joy and connection, for many parents, planning daily meals can be monotonous or stressful, made even more challenging when dealing with the unpredictability of a toddler's reactions to foods. Some common reasons we may feel stressed by meal planning include time constraints, balancing children's (sometimes very limited) preferences with our desire to serve a broad range of nourishing foods, financial constraints, and fears that our child isn't consuming enough food or variety. Most kids express some pickiness at some time, and it's normal for a toddler's appetite to increase and decrease at different stages of development. However, if there is ever a concern that your child isn't growing in line with expectations or that their nutritional needs aren't being met, please consult with your pediatrician.

Even in ideal mealtime routines and settings, it can be a struggle to set reasonable expectations for "normal" toddler eating. You might feel offended or discouraged when your child refuses a meal that you put time, effort, and money into preparing, or feel stressed by the food waste when your child refuses a meal.

Likewise, you might be triggered by mealtime behaviors that you perceive to be disrespectful or inappropriate, like if your child gets up from their seat frequently, talks while chewing, spits out a disliked food, plays with their food, doesn't finish everything on their plate, or doesn't help with mealtime cleanup.

Often unintentionally, parents who feel stressed by food and mealtime habits may communicate that stress in a way that is counterproductive. When kids push back on mealtime expectations, we might disengage or give in to the child's demands, taking the path of least resistance. While it's absolutely normal to occasionally need to make adjustments or accommodations, a consistent pattern of permissiveness or coercion in addressing mealtime behaviors can backfire.

Practical Strategies to Try

- **Stock a smart pantry.** Fill your fridge and cabinets with nutritive foods that you want your kids to have access to, and limit the availability of less nutritive choices.
- **Create consistent routines.** Plan meals and snacks at predictable times with consistent expectations. If your child refuses to eat

during the typical mealtime or complains of hunger shortly after mealtimes, consider adjusting mealtime schedules or availability of snacks before or after meals.

- **Eat together whenever possible.** Children thrive on social connection, and meals can feel more enjoyable when families use that time to connect socially, transcending the pressure to eat.
- **Be present in the moment.** We can promote more connection when we keep phones and other distractions away from the table, modeling the social benefits of limiting distraction and increasing person-to-person engagement.
- **Model the behaviors you want to see in them.** Consider what other eating behaviors you're modeling for your children, whether intentional or not. Do your kids see you eating a wide range of nutritive foods? What types of eating behaviors do you model, such as showing enjoyment of what you eat?
- **Be conscientious about how you talk about food.** Kids pick up on adults' negative attitudes and actions toward food. Try your best to present new foods in a neutral, nonjudgmental way, without stress or pressure. Focus on descriptive language rather than categorizing certain foods as "good or bad" or "healthy or unhealthy." Instead of "Eat this carrot, it's good for you," try, "This carrot is orange and tastes sweet and crunchy." Using descriptive language keeps the conversation judgment-free and engages your toddler's curiosity.
- **Avoid "always/never" thinking and language.** This leaves room for flexibility and changes in preference. This might look like "You didn't like the broccoli today. You might like it next time." Model flexible ways of eating ("I like dipping my broccoli in soy sauce to make it extra tasty for me") and normalize food preferences changing ("I don't like yogurt *yet*"), which leaves an opening to try the food again in the future.

- **Watch for fullness and hunger cues.** Rather than trying to force your child to "take one more bite" or "finish everything on your plate," prompt them to check in with their body by asking something like, "Do you want more dinner, or is your belly full?"
- **Offer choices.** You can support your children's autonomy within the environmental limits, rules, and boundaries you set. Offer choices within the options presented. This might also include presenting choices for serving foods in ways that align with personal preferences, like offering ketchup or other dips, or choosing where to put each food on the plate. Involve kids in food preparation or planning, whether that means getting their input in menu planning ("You get to choose our family's dinner tonight! Should we have pasta with meatballs or chicken?") or including them in grocery shopping. Encourage them to pick out a new fruit or vegetable at the grocery store and incorporate it into a meal.
- **Include teaching moments.** When talking about food, engage and educate your child by talking about specific nutritional qualities or the benefits of eating certain foods ("Chicken has protein that helps your muscles grow strong so you can run fast! Orange foods like carrots help you see in the dark!") See page 194 for resources on how to support your toddler's nutrition education.
- **Highlight positivity and playfulness.** Use positive language, including encouragement and praise, to reinforce your child's efforts to try new foods and appropriate mealtime behavior ("Thanks so much for staying in your seat at the table! Great job trying that broccoli today"). Embrace playfulness in mealtimes, like encouraging interest in a range of foods with "rainbow plates," seeing how many different-colored food kids can include on their plates.

Other Common Struggles

What if my kid keeps playing with food, dumping it, etc.?

Playing with food is developmentally appropriate for toddlers (maddening as it can be sometimes!), and you can set rules around if and when food play is acceptable. Remind them of the rules, boundaries, and consequences. This might look like, "Food stays on the table. Fork stays on the plate or in your mouth. If you dump your food on the floor, that tells me you're all done," and take food away if they persist. Prepare for pushback. If they are still hungry, remind them again of the rules and consequences, ensure they understand, and then provide immediate and frequent praise for following the rules ("Great job keeping your food on your plate!"). If they continue breaking the rule, remove the food again and hold your boundary. Also note that although many toddlers can learn to use utensils, you can allow them to eat with their fingers to help promote positive association with food.

What if my kid struggles with appropriate mealtime behaviors, like constantly getting up from the table or talking with food in their mouth?

For an active toddler, sitting to eat for more than five minutes may not be realistic. Consider whether your mealtime behavioral expectations are developmentally appropriate, and adjust them as needed. Use selective attention by praising appropriate mealtime behaviors and underreacting or ignoring minor misbehaviors (like talking with food in their mouth). You can also provide a simple rationale to explain the alternate behavior, like "I really want to hear what you're telling me, but I can't understand you." Use tools like a visual timer, playful games, or if-then positive consequences ("If you can stay in your seat until the timer rings, then we can read an extra book after breakfast") to shape mealtime behaviors.

What do I do about picky eating?

Picky eating is often a normal part of toddler development. Sometimes pickiness can be driven by a child's efforts to exert control, and parental pressure can contribute to increased stress and power struggles. The best strategy here is to model the eating habits you'd like your toddler to develop. Continue to expose them to foods they may have rejected in the past, and encourage even minimal efforts to engage with non-preferred foods (such as having it on the same plate as preferred foods, even if they don't eat it). Model that people can change their minds, such as "At first I didn't want green beans, but I changed my mind and decided to try it." Avoid punishing kids for not eating ("If you don't finish everything on your plate, you won't get bedtime stories"). There are many reasons why a child may not be eating, like changing appetite, sensory sensitivities, and personal preferences, and unrelated punishments don't address the problem. If your child's picky eating rises to a level of severity where their growth or nutritional needs are impacted, or social functioning is affected (for example, only eats in the presence of a parent who prepares food a particular way and refuses to eat with other caregivers) over an extended period of time, consult with your pediatrician.

What about using foods as rewards?

Using food as a reward or leverage can suggest that certain foods are more desirable than others, like that a cookie is a prize to be earned after reluctantly eating vegetables. Instead, focus on teaching kids what different kinds of foods offer to their bodies. Desserts are tasty and enjoyable, and it's great to have foods for the sake of joy, just like it's great to have foods for the sake of gaining energy and growth. Some parents choose to offer a dessert alongside other foods, presenting dessert as part of a well-rounded diet, permitting kids to choose when they eat each food within their meal. Parents who provide dessert at the end of a meal can use mindful language to talk about each foods' purpose and your child's internal cues ("When you fill your belly with foods that give you energy and strength, then you can have dessert") rather than using dessert coercively as a contingency or punishment ("You have to finish everything on your plate to have dessert" or "You hit your brother, so no dessert for a week").

My kid only sits long enough to eat if they are watching TV or an iPad. Is this harmful?

In the short term, devices can be a helpful distraction for getting kids to sit long enough to eat. In the long term, distractions at mealtimes can inhibit kids' abilities to develop the self-awareness skills they are meant to learn in the early childhood years. That said, sometimes parents need a break and a quick solution. If more often than not, you're able to use the proactive tools in this chapter to support your child's development through eating routines, it's reasonable to occasionally use a device to get through a tough day. If you find that you're primarily relying on devices to get through mealtimes, it will be effortful but worth the long-term benefits to do a reset on mealtime routines and expectations.

Useful Reminders and Reframes

The following reminders and reframes can help encourage parents who are concerned by their toddler's struggles.

- I worry about my child's eating because I want her to be healthy, and I know this one meal won't make or break her health.
- Rejecting the food I serve is not a rejection of me. Do not take this personally. This is not about me.
- It's okay if he feels a little hungry later. He will be okay if he refuels tomorrow.

Sleeping

A Practical Overview

Authoritative parents approach toddler sleep with the same formula as the other parenting situations—with a balance of warmth and connection, firm limits, and consistent boundaries. Family sleep practices are influenced by culture; individual characteristics, like the child's temperament; and family systems, like daily routines, parental stress, and dynamics of shared caregiving responsibilities in bedtime and daytime care. Although many families approach sleep practices differently in relation to bed or room sharing, sleep training, routines, etc., sleep impacts every family member and is a focus of general family health and well-being.

The National Sleep Foundation recommends that children 1 and 2 years old get 11 to 14 hours of sleep a day, and children 3 to 5 years old get 10 to 13 hours of sleep a day, inclusive of both nighttime sleep and naps. Research consistently demonstrates the importance of sleep for learning, as well as for social-emotional, behavioral, and physical health needs, and that poor sleep quality is associated with problems in learning and emotion and behavior regulation.

When deciding how to address your child and family's sleep needs, consider your personal, familial, and cultural values. If the sleep routines in your household are working for you, then great, keep it up! However, poor-quality child sleep can negatively impact parent sleep, which contributes to parental depression, anxiety, stress, low marital satisfaction, and increased conflict. If your sleep routines aren't working for you, your child, or your family, consider reassessing through an authoritative parenting lens—we'll explore how shortly.

Child's Perspective and Challenges

Toddlers are constantly moving, learning, and growing, which contributes to both the necessity of high-quality sleep as well as some challenges associated with sleep during this developmental period. For some kids, daytime curiosities and anxieties can carry over into the nighttime. A child may have learned a new skill that they want to practice in their bed at night, or they may think about a worry or a scary experience from daytime when it's time to sleep.

Separation fears are also normal and developmentally appropriate for this age. Toddlers may have difficulty transitioning to bed because they're eager for more connection time with caregivers, or they worry about missing out on nighttime activities that other family members are doing. Some toddlers also fear the experience of losing control by falling asleep. Rituals and routines help mitigate the effects of toddler fears. With predictable routines, kids learn they can cope with the worries that interfere with sleep, and that they'll be okay the next day. Unpredictable routines can contribute to anxiety or a sense of unsettledness, which interferes with the body's and mind's readiness for sleep. We'll explore all of this, too.

Parent's Perspective and Needs

Parents: We need sleep! It can be incredibly frustrating and stressful if our toddler's sleep behaviors don't align with ours, whether they're an early riser or late-night party animal. When kids have trouble falling asleep, our precious bit of time to ourselves is disrupted. We can feel frustrated and burnt-out when our kids' bedtime pushback creeps into our personal time. When we're sleep-deprived, it's harder to respond to our child calmly and skillfully. We're then more likely to react with anger or take shortcuts that the well-rested version of ourself has promised not to give in to (like allowing our child to sleep in our bed following a midnight wake-up, after we promised ourself not to!).

In many ways, it's evolutionarily adaptive for parents to have a strong reaction to a toddler's nighttime cries. Is the cry signaling severe distress? Concerns of safety or survival? It can be challenging to balance responding to sleep issues in ways that address the urgent need to just get back to sleep, while also supporting the development of the child's coping skills, resilience, and sleep health.

Practical Strategies to Try

- **Solidify daytime and nighttime routines.** As much as possible, try to maintain the same order of steps. Kids feel comforted in knowing what will come next, and over time, regular routines reduce the mental load on parents. Quiet nighttime rituals, such as a bath, stories, songs, and books, can help prepare your toddler's body and mind for sleep. Try to keep routines consistent across caregivers and different sleep settings. Familiar sleep rituals can communicate comfort and security despite changes in routines and environments.
- **Keep bedtime warm and positive.** Bedtime routines that also include predictable time for parent-child connection can help fill up your child's connection reserves before bed. Ideally, bedtime interactions are warm and positive, with minimal conflict. Realistically, there will be nights where this is challenging! As much as possible, stick to your routines, spend time connecting, and try to let go of frustrations that may have built up over the course of the day.
- **Assess the environment.** How might your toddler's sleep environment be contributing to sleep habits? Consider noise, temperature, light, and the presence of comfort objects. Think about whether your toddler would benefit from a white noise machine, blackout curtains, additional comfort objects (or fewer, if the bed's getting too crowded). For kids sharing a room with another family member, consider designating each person's sleep space, such as with

room dividers or curtains to create physical barriers. OK-to-wake clocks use different-colored lights to provide visual cues to toddlers that indicate when it's time to sleep or wake, which can also help toddlers learn to stay in bed until wake-up time after transitioning out of their cribs.

- **Express confidence and encourage coping.** Whereas younger babies rely heavily on their parents for soothing, parents can begin teaching toddlers how to cope with bedtime and sleep challenges. During the day, teach your toddler what they can do if they wake up to help them fall back asleep or feel calm. Practice calming skills, like hugging their stuffed animals, singing quietly to themselves, and using reassuring self-talk, like "I'm okay. I will see my grown-up in the morning." Remind your child about the calming skills before bed in a positive way, such as "Remember, you have Stuffie with you and he loves you. Give each other hugs." Praise their ability to practice calming skills, saying things like, "Great job finding a way to play quietly in your bed to feel calm!"

- **Phrase expectations positively.** During the day, use positive language to explain and practice sleep expectations, like "Stay in your bed" instead of "Don't climb out of bed." Describe what behaviors are appropriate and encouraged, such as using a quiet voice, using calming skills, and playing quietly with toys. When kids follow the expectations, make sure to express enthusiastic specific praise, like "Thanks so much for using your quiet voice in your bedroom!"

- **Plan ahead.** If you and your child are struggling with frequent wake-ups or difficulty falling asleep, work with your child to create a coping plan. During the day, tell your child the story of the problem, and coach them: "Let's practice covering yourself with the blanket so you don't need me to do it for you at night" or "Look for your sippy cup on the nightstand whenever you get thirsty." Asking for your child's input helps meet their drive for autonomy and control. As the wise parent, you can also offer suggestions and choices to guide them toward appropriate tools and skill development, particularly for younger toddlers who may not yet have the skills to identify helpful tools. Practice new skills during the day with dolls or stuffed animals. Remind your child of the plan when you say good night, and again if you need to go into their room later. Remember to shower them with specific praise for using their new skills!

Other Common Struggles

We've established regular routines and a restful sleep environment, but we're still facing challenges. What's going on?

It's normal for families to go through periods of challenges with sleep habits, even with a consistent routine in place. Some toddlers seem to find no better time in the day to try to assert their independence than when parents are trying to get them to sleep. Use strategies for supporting their autonomy by offering choices ("Which pajamas do you want to wear tonight—trucks or animals?"). Offer related rewards for compliance using "when/if-then" statements ("If you put on pajamas quickly, then we'll have time for an extra book"). Consider whether you need to make adjustments to routines, like dropping or shortening naps, or start the bedtime routine sooner to allow more time to wind down and connect.

How can we address bedtime pushback or nighttime wake-ups?

Create a coping plan during the day for how to respond. In a two-parent household, try to coordinate with your partner to ensure consistency. Plan ahead to determine which caregiver will respond each night so each parent also has protected sleep time when possible. Consider any needed adjustments to the daytime routine, like shifting the timing or length of naps to not interfere with nighttime sleep. For kids who don't seem tired at bedtime, ensure plenty of physical activity during the day, then transition to calming rituals an hour before bed.

My toddler sometimes resists his nap, even though he clearly needs one. What can I do?

Do your best to consistently set your toddler down for a nap, even if he refuses to sleep. You can phrase it as "quiet time" and point out some quiet, restful things he can do while in bed, like looking at a book or talking to his toys. This way, you are maintaining that consistent rest routine, whether or not he ends up falling asleep. You may also consider shifting bedtime earlier or later to see if a schedule change helps his body adapt. Conversely, parents may recognize their preschooler's need to drop a nap in order to improve nighttime sleep, but this may conflict with a daycare's naptime routines. Try to coordinate with daycare providers to offer alternate quiet-time activities that keep your child from napping during the day and increase their sleep needs at night.

My child just started preschool and has had a few nightmares lately. Are these events related?

Nightmares can be reactions to changes in daily routines, starting school, watching a high-stimulation TV show or movie, or experiencing stress, like at a doctor's appointment. Recognize that nightmares are relatively common and temporary. You can respond to your child with comfort, reassurance, and reminders of coping and calming skills. During the day, talk to your toddler about nightmares being pretend. You can also help them think about how to turn something from a scary nightmare into a playful, silly image to help them revise the narrative ("Imagine if instead of chasing you, that scary monster turned into a bubble and floated away!").

We changed our child's schedule to help her fall asleep, so why is bedtime even more challenging now?

You might find that by changing your routines or your responses to your toddler's sleep issues, the problem seems to only get worse. Remember the concept of the extinction burst from chapter 2—when changing boundaries, routines, or how you respond to your child's behavior, you can expect behaviors to get worse before they get better. This is a normal, predictable response to your child testing new limits. Allow yourself several days to consistently implement the new routine before assessing how effective it is—it usually takes both children and parents several days (or sometimes longer) to adjust. Ultimately, consistency in holding boundaries with a loving stance is key.

Useful Reminders and Reframes

The following reminders and reframes can help encourage parents who are concerned by their toddler's struggles.

- It's normal to have some tough nights of sleep. It's no one's fault.
- I can survive a few nights of poor sleep in the service of helping my child learn new sleep skills.
- We'll all feel better in the long term. We all deserve to feel well rested.

Toileting

A Practical Overview

For many families, toilet training is one of the first opportunities to teach our child a specific skill. Although there are varying approaches to toilet training, authoritative parents can use the same general framework to approach this parenting task: with a combination of supportive presence with firm boundaries and limits. While this chapter provides a general overview, check out the resource list (page 194) for more helpful resources on toddler toileting.

Toddlers benefit from meeting certain physiological, motor, and psychological milestones of readiness before beginning toilet training. To learn to use the toilet, kids need to have an awareness of their body's signal of the urge to pee or poop and to have developed an ability to delay the release of pee or poop long enough to get to the toilet. Kids might show these signs of awareness by touching their diaper, or grunting or squatting when trying to poop.

Development of motor skills also helps with toileting readiness, like walking with enough coordination to get to the bathroom, getting on and off the potty, and pushing down pants. Cognitively, kids need to connect the dots between the physical sensation of needing to go and following through on getting to the bathroom without distraction. Kids may also show readiness through social motivation, like expressing an interest in using the potty like other kids they know, and through their emotional drive for independence. Although not every milestone *needs* to be met, toilet training is easier when many of these developmental foundations are in place.

Child's Perspective and Challenges

Some kids are eager for the independent, "big-kid" experience of using a toilet, whereas others may seem indifferent or totally uninterested. Many toddlers are socially motivated and want to imitate what they see caregivers, older siblings, or peers do.

Toddlers may experience emotional barriers to toileting. When caregiver expectations exceed a child's abilities, they may feel distressed, frustrated, and discouraged and may experience low self-esteem. Toddlers might feel afraid of the *whoosh* of water disappearing down the pipes, evoking fears of whether they, too, might disappear down the drain. Particularly when it comes to pooping in the toilet, some toddlers feel they are losing a physical part of themselves and are afraid to release. It's also common for busy toddlers to be distractible during daytime activities, which can interfere with their ability to recognize body signals and initiate using the bathroom.

Parent's Perspective and Needs

Often, the focus of potty-training readiness is on the child's milestones. Yet as parents, our readiness is equally, if not more, important. We may be ready to teach sooner than our child is ready to learn, for reasons like pressure from friends and family, or eagerness to transition out of diapers to save money or resources, or even to prevent persistent diaper rash. On the other hand, sometimes parents hesitate to start potty training, regardless of the child's readiness. Some parents see the effort involved in potty training as daunting or find diapers to be more convenient—less stress about accidents on the go and the ease of not needing to be on top of a newly potty-trained toddler's every move.

Potty training can be stressful for many parents. You might not think you have the time to devote to teaching, or you may feel like you don't have the skills to calmly and confidently teach your child how to use the bathroom. You may worry, *What if she doesn't pick up on potty training? What if he's not ready? I don't want to deal with the mess of accidents. I'm not ready to let go of this baby phase.* And once you start the potty-training process, you may feel frustrated by a lack of progress or a sense of doubt that your child will ever stop using diapers or having accidents. These are all common concerns. Patience is key, so hang in there.

Practical Strategies to Try

- **Build body awareness.** Even before you begin potty training, start familiarizing your child with different parts of the process by helping them build body awareness. Describe your observations of peeing and pooping behaviors in their diaper. Be on the lookout for certain facial expressions or body movements. Some kids may instinctively retreat to a special spot to hide when trying to poop in their diaper. A simple label, like "Jordan is pooping," helps kids associate body sensations with communication. Their behaviors are reinforced by your interest and attention. If your toddler verbalizes that they have a dirty diaper, enthusiastic praise will reinforce their awareness and communication through your positive attention ("Great job listening to your body! Thank you for telling me!"). Conversely, avoid negative words that may elicit shame ("Ew, gross, that stinks!").
- **Use modeling to normalize the use of the bathroom.** When toddlers see their parents and siblings in the routine of using the bathroom (when appropriate) and washing hands, the process becomes familiar and they're more likely to feel comfortable and want to imitate. It can even be helpful, after changing your toddler's diaper, to practice taking your toddler to the bathroom to help you dump the poop from the diaper into the toilet, flush, and say, "Bye-bye, poop!" so they become more comfortable with understanding where poop goes after it leaves the body. Kids learn better when concepts are presented concretely. Real-life examples like this, as well as books and practice with toys, can help build your child's understanding.

- **Set realistic expectations for the transition from diapers to potty use.** Be mindful of your child's specific developmental needs, abilities, strengths, and limitations. If parents' expectations are too high, kids are left feeling discouraged and frustrated by their inability to meet the demands. Consider yourself and your limits. If you feel stressed by potty training, turn to your social circles for advice, venting, and support. Of course, every child is different and every family is different, so what worked for your friends' kids might or might not work for yours.
- **Expect and plan for accidents.** When they happen, do all you can to react neutrally. Avoid shame and blame. Focus on a gentle reminder that "Pee and poop go in the potty." It's important to know that daytime toilet training can be taught, whereas nighttime dryness is a biological process that develops over time, at different ages for different kids.
- **When feasible, use a potty designed for toddlers.** This will help your child learn by reducing barriers to success. Toddler potties are designed to be the right size for their body, which lessens the fear of falling in, and the stability of keeping their feet on the floor reduces the need for physical exertion that can feel unfamiliar and challenging.
- **Integrate bathroom use into daily routines.** Guide them to the bathroom before sleep and upon waking, when leaving the house, and before watching TV and other activities that may be hard for kids to stop independently or that may distract kids from body awareness.
- **Maintain your warm, loving, and supportive stance.** Offer lots of behavior-specific praise and encouragement. Throughout the process, communicate your confidence in your child's ability to learn something new. Praise process, not perfection. If your child tells you they have to pee but they don't make it to the bathroom

in time, you can say, "Thank you for telling me you needed to go." If some pee dribbles on the floor, compliment what they did well, and encourage them to help wipe up the dribbles.

Other Common Struggles

Our toddler is using the toilet at home but having accidents at preschool. What can we do?

Other caregivers, like co-parents, babysitters, or daycare teachers, may disagree about how to approach toileting issues and may have different rules and routines. Talk with other caregivers to get on the same page about how you would like everyone to approach toileting with your child, aiming to maintain as much consistency as possible between settings. When there are disagreements, set a neutral time to talk with other caregivers about each perspective, and work to find alignment for the sake of your child's developmental needs. Explicitly discuss the barriers and challenges that each caregiver anticipates, and make a plan in advance for how those concerns will be handled. If it's impossible to find agreement between caregivers (for example, some parents avoid pull-ups entirely, while some daycares require pull-ups to a certain age or milestone), talk to your child in advance about similarities and differences between settings and caregivers so they know what to expect. Try to keep the message positive and encouraging.

My kid and I are in constant power struggles about using the bathroom. How can we find common ground?

Toddlers and preschoolers assert their need for control in toileting just as they do in many other situations. Parents may struggle to find the balance between prompting their child to use the bathroom and relying on the child to self-initiate. Toileting is a big step toward independence. Allow your child to feel in control. This will help them gain the full independence to be in charge of their bodily needs and toileting routines. If you know your child has to go and is refusing, try to influence their behavior by offering choices ("Do you want to use the toddler potty or the grown-up toilet?") and naming natural positive and negative consequences ("If you try to use the potty now, we will have extra time to play. If you don't use the potty now, you might feel uncomfortable during playtime and it might not be as fun"). Ultimately, kids are in control of when they release pee and poop—even if you physically held them down—so try to stay calm and neutral. Likewise, when accidents happen, recognize that the accident is a natural consequence and part of their learning process. Involve them in cleanup to teach responsibility, without resorting to blame and shame.

My kid had solid toileting skills, but lately they've been having accidents. What's going on?

Toileting regressions can happen, often in reaction to changes in routine or a stressor (such as a new daily schedule, school break, travel, new baby at home, new school, or illness). If you can't identify a reason for the regression, consider consulting with your pediatrician to rule out any physical causes. In the meantime, remain encouraging and confident in their abilities. As much as possible, reinforce expectations and try to maintain consistent and familiar routines, like reminding them to try the potty at predictable times in the daily routine, and making the toddler potty more accessible as a physical reminder to go. For your well-being, remind yourself that regressions are temporary.

My child does fine with pee, but poop is a struggle! What can we do to help?

Common poop struggles include holding poop in, refusing to poop in the toilet, and only pooping in a pull-up or nighttime diapers. This can happen due to fears of releasing into the abyss of a toilet bowl instead of the comfort of a diaper, or as an effort to exert control. After ruling out any physiological causes and consequences of withholding (like constipation) with a pediatrician, parents can use behavioral interventions that focus on scaffolding, or gradually fading support. For example, your toddler poops in their pull-up while standing in the bathroom? Awesome! One step closer. Sits on the potty while wearing a pull-up to poop? Great—even closer! See page 114 for additional resources on this subject. No matter what, remind yourself this is all part of the process, and with patience, your toddler will eventually learn to be independent in the bathroom.

Useful Reminders and Reframes

The following reminders and reframes can help encourage parents who are concerned by their toddler's struggles.

- This is part of their learning process. He is not trying to make life harder for me. The challenges are not his fault.
- I can be proud of progress, even though we still have a long way to go.
- She will eventually learn to use the toilet. This is hard now, and I can stay committed to help us all get to the other side.

Learning

A Practical Overview

As children enter the toddler years, parents have more opportunities to teach new skills and help them learn. Much of a young child's learning occurs through the context of play and within relationships. Some parents approach parenting toddlers with ideas of many lessons and skills they want to teach—from life skills, like how to crack an egg, to academic skills, like recognizing letters and sounds, to social skills, like how to share toys with other kids. Our teaching goals are informed by our cultural influences, parenting values, and beliefs about child development and learning. Some parents may view their role in their child's learning as less active, relying more on school settings, natural processes, or exposure to other experiences to help their kids learn.

Authoritative parents can use a balance of warmth and limits to support the development of their toddlers' autonomy, self-exploration, and development of cognitive skills. There's a time and a place for parents to set up opportunities for unstructured free play, as well as times for more explicit parental instruction. Both are necessary for children's learning. Independent play within the limits established by caregivers supports development of children's autonomy, self-regulation, confidence, and independence in problem-solving skills. Explicit teaching from parents is also necessary at times to help kids develop the skills they need to be confident and competent.

Let this be another reminder that not every interaction with your child needs to be a teachable, meaningful moment! When parents create a supportive environment in which toddlers can explore, so much learning happens naturally. Release any sense of pressure put on by yourself, family, or community that constant adult intervention is required for learning. Think holistically about the balance of learning opportunities you provide to your kids over time. A balance of independent and adult-led interactions is essential for developing resilient learners—the kind of learners with grit and curiosity who can push through challenges.

Child's Perspective and Challenges

Toddlers are naturally curious and eager to learn. They also develop a greater sense of autonomy and confidence when provided with opportunities to explore their interests. In fact, learning is more powerful when it takes place in the natural environment and meets the child where their abilities and interests are.

Depending on individual characteristics like personality and activity level, some kids may have an easier time sitting and paying attention long enough to learn a specific skill. When trying to learn something new, kids may feel frustrated or discouraged when the outcome doesn't match the expectations, or when parents' expectations exceed the child's abilities.

Has your child ever built a block tower and then, when a few pieces toppled, deliberately knocked the whole building down, confusingly making the situation worse for themselves? Frustration is part of the learning process, and we can support them in coping to help them develop frustration tolerance and self-regulation, setting a strong foundation for coping with challenges in future learning situations.

Parent's Perspective and Needs

Particularly in our current information-loaded, competitive culture, parents often feel pulled to turn every moment into a teachable moment. Some parents are influenced by social comparisons and pressure to teach certain skills. When they hear that their child's classmate learned how to ride a bike, they may feel the pressure to keep up and push their child to do the same.

When you're teaching your child a new skill, you might feel uncomfortable seeing them struggle and feel an urge to jump in and solve the problem for them. However, there are benefits to allowing kids to struggle within reason, including learning problem-solving skills, building confidence and a sense of competence, and coping with frustration. Some parents may also feel uncomfortable with messes or failure, which can get in the way of autonomy-supportive teaching. For example, a parent who wants to teach their child how to crack an egg but is grossed out just anticipating the mess of a ruptured yolk dripping off the countertop, might overly intervene. Such intrusive involvement communicates a lack of confidence in a child's abilities and prevents a child from learning and growing from mistakes, while also limiting their exploration of a wide range of interests.

You can enlist your own coping skills to help you tolerate any discomfort of watching your kid struggle or make a mess when learning something new, keeping your eye on the prize of the immense pride everyone feels when kids overcome a challenge and develop a new skill.

Practical Strategies to Try

- **Provide plenty of opportunities for unstructured free play.** Join in their play world, and know that child-led free play (see "Fill Connection Reserves," page 53) helps kids learn self-regulation and problem-solving skills that will serve them throughout their life. You can also incorporate any other skills you want to teach through the natural play environment. When following along with your child's play, you might count aloud as you observe them place one block on top of another, or label the colors and shapes that they're sorting, integrating foundational school-readiness skills into play.

- **Scaffold with "show me, guide me, help me, let me."** When teaching a new skill, help kids move from dependence to independence by providing hands-on support as needed, then gradually reducing your involvement. Take the example of teaching your child how to crack an egg:
    - **Show me:** Model a new skill while describing what you are doing. For example, "I tap the egg gently on the counter until I see a crack. I hold it over the bowl. I pull the shell apart and let the insides pour in. I hold the shell the whole time."
    - **Guide me:** Use hands-on support to guide your child to practice a new skill, perhaps placing your hand on top of your child's to complete the task together. For example, "I'll help you hold the egg. Now we tap it gently, just like that. Look, we made a crack! Now we carefully hold it over the bowl to pull the shell apart."
    - **Help me:** Provide assistance as needed. Give reminders of how to complete the task or with partial hands-on support while expressing confidence in your child's ability to work through the task independently. For example, "You try it now. Remember to tap lightly. I'm here if you need help. You can do it!"
    - **Let me:** Allow your child to complete the task independently. Provide encouragement and compliments for effort. Accept imperfection. For example, "Great, you did it all by yourself! A little piece of shell fell in the bowl. That's okay. We can use a spoon to scoop it out."
- **Work together with "I start, you finish."** Break new skills into small, reasonable chunks so it's more likely your child will be successful, and share the load. Complete part of the task for your child to gain cooperation and set up a more realistic goal. For example, when teaching your toddler how to put on socks independently,

say and model, "I start," doing the first step for them, followed by "you finish," to guide them to pull their sock over the rest of their foot. Or reverse to say, "You start, I finish."

- **Map out a plan.** When trying to teach something new, give yourself enough time, plan ahead, and have appropriate materials available to reduce stress. If you're teaching your child how to crack an egg for a recipe, have them practice in a separate bowl so if the outcome isn't as planned, you can easily correct and move forward with the recipe. You know your child best, so set realistic expectations for what your child is ready to learn.
- **Praise process.** Provide positive feedback for behaviors that demonstrate learning steps on the way to reaching the full goal. The first time your child cracks an egg, they will almost certainly get shell in the bowl or egg white on the countertop. This is still worthy of praise: Even imperfectly, they were able to independently practice a new skill! By praising their efforts and what they did well, they'll be more eager to practice and learn to improve.

Other Common Struggles

My three-year-old expresses fear about learning new skills that I want her to learn, like swimming. What should I do?

Ease in with loving encouragement and an expression of confidence. Avoiding a situation that your child is afraid of will reinforce her fears, communicating that the situation is truly something to be afraid of, even when it's not. Adjust your goals and expectations, and supportively encourage your child to work toward a goal that is a small step outside their comfort zone, on their way to the larger learning goal. This might look like sitting on the pool stairs with her and letting her dangle her feet in the water while watching the other children.

On the flip side, maybe you recognize that your three-year-old is ready and eager to learn to swim, but your discomfort around swimming is likely to make everyone feel more stressed and interfere with your child's learning. Check in with your own tolerance and limitations. Ask yourself if you can cope with the imperfections involved in teaching a new skill. When needed, rely on co-parents, other caregivers, or specialized instructors to help your child learn when your own discomforts get in the way.

I feel pressured to teach my child to read before school starts, but I don't have that kind of patience. How can I find a balance that works for me?

It's good to recognize and honor your limits regarding what you want or need to teach as a parent. It's not necessarily a parent's job to teach kids how to read, for example, but you can influence reading skill development by emphasizing a love of learning and integrating related practices at home. Playing rhyming games, reading together daily, keeping books at home, visiting the library, and modeling by sharing your interest in reading will help your child with reading readiness for school learning, without having to focus too much on teaching the mechanics of sounding out words and the like.

My child always asks for help with tasks he's done successfully many times. Why is this?

Some kids heavily rely on adult intervention and support, and may constantly ask for help, even for tasks you know they're capable of. Sometimes requests for help are a request for attention and connection in disguise, or a low frustration tolerance, rather than a lack of ability. Take a kid asking for help opening a toy bin. Before jumping in to solve the situation for them, connect through validation and encourage them to try two times on their own first, providing enthusiastic praise for effort along the way. If they're able to open the bin, amazing! You've just helped build their confidence, adaptability, and persistence! Compliment them (and yourself!) for problem-solving and persistence. If they are unable to complete the task, help them and offer compliments for trying.

Why doesn't my child listen to me when I try to teach new skills?

This happens. Kids may push back on adult instruction when learning a new skill. Start by trying to identify the reason(s) behind the push-back. Is the expectation beyond their abilities? Are they worried about failure or disappointing you or themselves? Are they trying to assert autonomy? Is the task just boring? Once you identify possible reasons for pushback, find a solution that matches, whether it's to adjust expectations, validate their feelings, offer choices, or make learning activities more fun by incorporating your child's interests.

Useful Reminders and Reframes

The following reminders and reframes can help encourage parents who are concerned by their toddler's struggles.

- It's okay if they scrape their knee or make a mess. Imperfection is part of learning. Mistakes help us grow. This will help them build resilience and confidence through experience.
- Not every interaction with my child needs to be a meaningful, teachable moment.
- It's hard to see my child struggle, but I can cope. I can step back to let them try on their own before I jump in.

Socializing

A Practical Overview

Humans are inherently social creatures—we thrive on social engagement and connection. Some elements of social growth occur naturally through the course of development, while other social skills are shaped through experience in relationships and interactions in the environment. A toddler's natural curiosity may lead them to engage in behaviors that adults view as socially problematic, like grabbing toys or hugging peers without permission. Verbal behaviors parents may find to be socially offensive include not saying "please" and "thank you," or not giving an apology in the way we want them to.

Just as kids learn to talk or jump at different times, they also develop social skills at different times. For some kids, socializing comes naturally, while others need more hands-on support to learn social skills. All kids benefit from an authoritative parenting approach that focuses on modeling positive social behaviors in daily interactions, while providing a high level of warmth and maintaining developmentally appropriate boundaries around social expectations.

Use of positive discipline approaches (see "Learn to Influence Young Children's Behavior," page 61) over harsh, punitive approaches are associated with greater use of positive social skills in kids. Sometimes parents may be overly harsh without necessarily intending harm. For example, parents who highly value compliance and listening might intervene intrusively with their child's behaviors in order to force compliance, at the expense of supporting their autonomy and skill development. For authoritative parents, the goal is to set developmentally appropriate expectations and take an active role in helping their child develop social skills without overcontrolling and infringing on their autonomy.

Child's Perspective and Challenges

Kids are truly sponges. They soak up cues from their environments—from the language they hear to the social exchanges they witness. And while some social skills develop naturally during the early childhood years, kids are strongly influenced by the environments they participate in and the people around them. Kids often emulate the social interactions they observe, whether by comforting an upset friend the way they've been comforted, or by yelling and shouting in the ways they may have observed others reacting to conflict.

At this stage, toddlers are learning to understand other people's perspectives. Younger toddlers might not yet realize the impact of their actions on others, both positive and negative. Perspective-taking skills are a work in progress; they're also a key element to developing social skills.

As with all new skills, it can help to remember that limit testing and mistakes are part of learning, and the best learning takes place when kids can do so in the context of safe, reliable, comforting relationships and environments.

Parent's Perspective and Needs

As parents, we may struggle to balance the expectations we have for our children's social behavior with their actual abilities. Maybe we're unsure what is developmentally appropriate, wondering at what age or stage it's appropriate to expect kids to say please and thank you, or apologize, or take turns sharing with peers. We may feel embarrassed when our kids don't meet our social expectations, viewing poor manners as a reflection of our parenting or worrying that our child might be rude. It's easy for parents to fall into a negative belief trap that bad manners or uncooperative play in early childhood may be an unchangeable personality trait, fearing that their toddler who doesn't ask politely for a turn on the swing at the playground will become a friendless, verbally aggressive adult. Have no fear! What might seem like a series of social faux pas to us are very often typical toddler behaviors that will fade and evolve over time.

In all of this, parent the child you have and meet them where they are. Reflect on your social values and goals, and check in to see if these are realistic for your child at the stage they're in. Amid your efforts to raise kind and resilient kids, show kindness and compassion toward yourself first. It will carry over into your relationship with your child and ultimately into your child's relationship with others.

Practical Strategies to Try

- **Emphasize emotions.** Emotional awareness is one of the core foundational skills to promote positive social behaviors. When you use emotion-focused language in daily activities, you help your child learn about their emotions and the emotions of others, which will help develop their perspective-taking abilities. When reading books or watching a show, talk about the emotions of the characters you observe, such as "He looks so sad" or "Look, she is surprised!" When kids are able to see situations from others' point of view, they start to notice other people's needs and are more likely to engage in using kind language and manners, taking turns, and offering help. You can also bring your child's attention to facial reactions and body language. By pairing language with nonverbal communication, you'll help build your child's awareness of other people's feelings and the impact of their actions on others. Help them notice when a peer on the playground walks toward them with a smile, maybe indicating an interest in playing, or when their younger sibling cries after they grab a toy from them, showing they feel hurt by their big sibling's actions. Review chapter 3 for tips on supporting emotional development.
- **Consider the environment and the social interactions your kids witness.** It's important to consider the behaviors we're modeling.

Harsh discipline, like corporal punishment or yelling and name-calling, communicates to a child that hitting or name-calling are acceptable ways to solve problems (while we know they are not), and that will likely be how kids try to solve problems with peers. We can ask ourselves how we are modeling kindness and respect. Even in the context of, for example, driving in traffic: Ask yourself, *When someone cuts me off, how do I react, and what might my child be learning from my response?*

- **Practice social skills in play.** Special playtime (page 54) is a great opportunity to use child-led play to model, practice, and praise social skills at your child's developmental level, like taking turns, cooperating, paying compliments, and sharing. Create play situations to practice specific social skills, or use dolls or puppets to role-play.
- **Provide live feedback and opportunities for corrective behaviors.** One of the most powerful tools you can use is to bring attention to your child when they are engaging in appropriate social skills (rather than focusing attention only when things *aren't* going well). If you're constantly having to remind your kid to not grab toys from others, what's the positive opposite behavior you can be on the lookout for? Offer an enthusiastic compliment every time you notice your child waiting patiently or asking kindly for a turn. If you observe them grabbing a toy, instead of harshly reprimanding or letting it go, provide an immediate opportunity for corrective feedback, helping your child practice the appropriate alternative behavior ("I see you really want a turn with the fire truck. Please use calm and kind words to ask, 'Can I have a turn when you're done?' "). When they do so, even with your scripted support, offer enthusiastic praise.
- **Offer choices.** There are multiple options to participate in socially acceptable ways. Perhaps your child is shy and slow to warm up, so when a stranger compliments his cool light-up sneakers in the

grocery store, he buries his face in your leg. Parents who value saying please and thank you may try to force him to say thank you. Instead, try modeling expressing gratitude yourself and offer alternatives ("Thanks for the compliment! Joey, you can say thank you or you can give a thumbs-up to show thanks").

- **Resist the urge to use force, coercion, or punishment around enforcing socially appropriate behaviors.** Instead, use positive strategies for influencing behaviors (see pages 61–67), like proactive praise for positive opposites, "when/if-then" language, and immediate and related consequences when needed to help teach the skill. Remember, many social expectations we have as parents may not necessarily suit the developmental expectations of our toddlers.

Other Common Struggles

I want my child to say please and thank you, but it's not happening. Am I expecting too much?

Many caregivers struggle with social behaviors that don't meet their expectations or understanding of the child's developmental level and needs. With any challenging social behavior, first check your expectations and adjust as needed for developmental appropriateness. It may not be reasonable to expect kids to say please and thank you 100 percent of the time. Likewise, your expectation of how your child should express an apology may not match their temperament or skill level. Consider whether you can adjust your expectations to meet them where they are and help supportively shape them to the best version of themselves. In short, focus your feedback on the behavior, rather than the child being a problem.

Why is my child always lying, even when there's no apparent reason for it?

Lying or fibbing is a common socially inappropriate behavior for adults that actually may be developmentally appropriate for kids! Consider the reason behind the behavior. A child who lies about feeling sick or hurt may be trying to avoid an activity they don't want to do or seek connection and comfort from a caregiver. A child who rips up their sibling's artwork and then denies it may feel afraid of getting in trouble or embarrassed about doing something they realize is wrong.

To help kids learn to be honest, we can create an environment where they feel safe to share mistakes and talk about misbehaviors. Lead with connection. Use calm, curious, and open language ("I wonder how Jake's drawing got to be in so many pieces"). If and when your child acknowledges responsibility, thank them for their honesty. This communicates comfort and safety in being honest, making it more likely they'll be honest in the future. If the lie is related to a behavior that requires a consequence, choose a consequence that is immediate and related, like helping repair the torn drawing (see "Correcting a Child's Behavior," page 67).

Toddlers and preschoolers may also lie as a way of expressing a fantasy or a wish. Although it's common for kids at this stage to occasionally blur the line between fantasy and reality, caregivers can help model and clarify this distinction; first by repeating the child's statement to help the child feel seen and connected, then by distinguishing between truths and wishes. For example, "Wow, that would be so cool to have a dinosaur visit your classroom! Is that something that really happened, or that you wish could happen?"

How can I respond when my child doesn't want to interact with certain family members or friends?

Occasionally, your parenting social values may not align with those of other family members or friends. Perhaps Grandpa comes to visit and insists on hugging your toddler, despite their protests, while you have been trying to teach them to ask for permission before touching or hugging others. When other people's social behaviors contradict the social messages you want to teach, intervene immediately by redirecting with words and actions in a toddler-friendly way, like "Grandpa, it looks like Sophie doesn't want a hug right now. We can wave to say hello instead." This demonstrates to your toddler consistency in your social message and protects her right to her personal space. If needed, follow up with the family or friend privately, outside the presence of your toddler, to explain your parenting intentions and boundaries, as well as your child's perspective on the issue.

Useful Reminders and Reframes

The following reminders and reframes can help encourage parents who are concerned by their toddler's struggles.

- I can model and support all the best social skills, and my child will still have moments when they struggle to share, cooperate, help, or speak kindly. I don't expect perfection.
- We are all fallible humans who do the best we can most of the time. Sometimes people say please; sometimes they don't. Sometimes they wait patiently for a turn; sometimes they don't.
- Like anything else, my child's social skills are under construction. Single interactions do not define my child forever.

Chapter 5

Specific Situations and Behaviors

This chapter serves as a resource for parents navigating some of the stormier waters of the toddler years, with the same authoritative balance of warmth and steady control that you've applied to the everyday routines. Although the specific situations and behaviors described in this chapter are common, they tend to be more complicated and emotional for families to navigate, including big transitions, such as introducing a new sibling into the family dynamic, and tricky situations, like going to the doctor for medical care.

- Big Changes at Home
- Doctor Visits and Medicine
- Pacifiers and Comfort Objects
- Starting New Childcare
- New Baby and Siblings
- Dealing with Fear and Anxiety
- Risky Play Versus Unsafe Behaviors
- Discussing Hard Topics Like Death

Big Changes at Home

A Practical Overview

Throughout a child's development, families go through many changes. Some are inevitable and seem routine, like a child transitioning from a crib to a toddler bed. Other changes may be unexpected, like a caregiver illness. Still others may be planned but significant, like a new baby, moving to a new home or town, changing schools, or parental divorce.

At times, it might seem easy to anticipate how your child will experience the change. A cross-country move, for example, is clearly a big change to the physical environments, people, and routines that your toddler will encounter every day. For other changes, it may be harder for parents to recognize the impact on a child. When a parent is starting a new job, for example, parents may assume that their toddler won't be affected if the new job doesn't impact the toddler's daily routines. However, toddlers can be sensitive to subtle changes in family dynamics, like shifts in parental stress and attention.

Although not every situation can be addressed specifically, the following section offers a general guide that can be applied across a range of contexts for parenting toddlers through big changes. The resource list on page 192 includes recommendations for further reading to address specific situations like parental conflict, separation anxiety, and more.

Child's Perspective and Challenges

Children thrive on predictability and routines, and they feel secure when they feel a sense of control in their environment. When changes happen and routines are disrupted, children may lose that sense of security. Children also pick up on the stress that we feel about changes. Children may perceive a difference in frequency or quality of their interactions with us, and without understanding these changes, they may feel confused or blame themselves. Especially when kids don't have the developmental ability to verbalize their feelings and questions, we might see changes in their behaviors that can pose even greater challenges for the family.

With proper preparation, children can better make sense of their internal experiences, like their feelings and narratives about the change, and environmental differences, like the practical changes in their routines and different interactions with caregivers. We'll explore some strategies shortly.

Parent's Perspective and Needs

Big changes at home often mean more stress for parents. If you're planning a move to a new home or job, you likely have less time, attention, and energy to put toward parenting. This is absolutely understandable! Recognize your bandwidth, and with that self-awareness, adjust accordingly. You might plan to be even more intentional about allocating your limited time at home and with your child. By acknowledging the reality of how a change impacts you, and integrating that with your understanding of your child's needs, you might adapt your approach to taking care of yourself, your child, and your household. By raising awareness of how changes—big or small—can impact your child, you can understand why they might be acting or feeling the way they do, and use the following strategies to address their needs.

Practical Strategies to Try

- **Talk about the change before it happens.** Take your child's perspective about how the change will impact them, and describe those expectations using child-friendly language. If a parent is starting a new job and won't be home when the child wakes up, your child may be wondering who they will see in the morning, who will get them ready for school, and when they'll see that parent next. Describe these changes simply, with a focus on what they can expect ("When Mommy leaves for work, Daddy will get you ready in the morning, and you will see Mommy when she comes home at dinnertime").

- **Be choosy about what you share.** Consider the amount of information your toddler is able to process at a given time, and share relevant information as needed. Be mindful about the conversations that your child may be overhearing. If your family is moving, but you're not yet sure when or where, it might not yet be time to discuss the change in front of your toddler, who may feel confused and unsettled by the uncertainty.
- **Use visual or concrete tools to help your child prepare for the change.** For example, if a parent is away on a business trip or you're preparing to move to a new home, you can create a simple countdown calendar that they can use to mark each passing day with a sticker, or a paper chain, where they can rip off a ring for each day of the countdown.
- **Create a coping plan.** Try to imagine how your child may feel about the changes, and practice ways they can cope with those feelings. You might show them a comforting toy they can hug, practicing aloud a positive reminder they can say to themselves ("I miss Mommy, and I'm excited to see her at dinnertime"), or talking about who they can go to if they need help. You can use dolls or stuffies to act out the situation and ways to cope with their feelings.
- **Talk about what's the same and what's a change.** Kids find comfort in the familiar. When talking about changes at home, also emphasize what will stay the same. Together, come up with a list of things that will stay the same and things that will change, or

turn it into a game called Same or Change. For example, when transitioning from a crib to a toddler bed, you might note that the changes are the new bed, new blankets, and new sheets; and things that stay the same are the room, Daddy coming in to wake them up, and the special bedtime stuffed animals. In the case of parental separation, you might explain to your toddler that what's staying the same is that both parents love and care for her and that she will bring her clothes and blankie between homes, and what's different is that she will take turns at each parent's home and will do activities with one parent at a time. Familiar items and routines amid the disruption of changes provide a sense of comfort and security to your children.

Other Common Struggles

We just moved to a new home, and it's been great, but our toddler is misbehaving more. What's going on?

Changes at home, whether big or small, can often lead to changes in children's behaviors. Behavior is communication. Even when kids express excitement or indifference about a change, it's common to see behavioral changes, like greater sleep disruption or challenges with sleep routines, clinginess or separation anxiety, pushback or oppositional behavior, or efforts to exert control in other areas, like eating. Remind yourself that this is very normal for young kids. Offer compassion to yourself and to your child. Do your best to maintain structure and routine. Incorporate special time (see "Fill Your Connection Reserves," page 53) to provide more connection and reinforce feelings of trust and security.

Behavior changes may also show up in contexts that seem unrelated to the change, like in daycare. Proactively communicate with other care providers to share what's going on at home and how your toddler may be affected. Although you don't need to share the specifics of personal family stressors or changes, even a brief heads-up that your child may be reacting to stress or change at home can be helpful. This open line of communication with other caregivers gives context to your child's behaviors and allows for partnership in supporting your child's needs.

My partner is recovering from surgery, and I'm stressed and exhausted. What can I do to maximize my limited time and energy resources?

Changes at home can often feel depleting for parents. If you're moving, changing jobs, or dealing with illness, your bandwidth might be severely limited. Recognize your limits, and lean on your social supports and coping skills to help regulate yourself (see "What to Do When You're Triggered," page 84). Consider quality over quantity of your parent-child interactions. Try to maintain routines and offer brief, high-quality one-on-one time with your child within the limits of your bandwidth.

If you can anticipate a change, try to soften the impact of the upcoming depletion by doing your best to make sure your family routines are set and your connection reserves are as full as they can be. Reset your expectations for yourself during times of change. Maybe that means setting a goal of functioning at 70 percent and accepting the reality when you're functioning at 50 percent.

In all of this, consider your own self-care needs. With your limited bandwidth and increased stress, you may have even less time to take care of yourself, despite these needs being even more pressing than usual. Make a self-care plan, using the strategies in "The Deal with Dysregulation," page 80.

My toddler is asking questions that I'm not sure how to answer. What do I do?

Toddlers are curious, and they may ask questions or express ideas about the change that you're not sure how to answer, either because you don't have a clear answer yet or the answer is emotionally loaded. It's okay to acknowledge that you're not sure or not ready to respond, which gives you more time to make sure that the information you share is accurate, appropriate, and helpful. In the meantime, validate your child's feelings and curiosities and communicate connection with supportive presence while addressing the lack of information ("I know you're wondering about that. I am, too. I'm not sure how to answer that yet. When I find the answer, I'll let you know. I'm here for you, and I love you"). See "Discussing Hard Topics Like Death," page 185, for additional guidance.

Useful Reminders and Reframes

The following reminders and reframes can help encourage parents who are concerned by their toddler's struggles.

- Change is hard, and it is temporary. Everything is a season, and seasons change.
- It may be hard right now to see through the other side, but eventually we will make it through and our routines will stabilize.
- We are adaptable, and we can cope.

Doctor Visits and Medicine

A Practical Overview

Even though doctor visits and medical care are a routine part of childhood, they can be quite challenging for families. For some children, medical visits occur relatively infrequently, but for others, medical needs are more frequent, complex, or unpredictable. As parents, our approach to handling challenging medical care needs with our child will depend on individual characteristics, like the child's temperament, their familiarity and past experiences with medical care, and other family and social factors.

Although kids may have mostly unremarkable experiences with medical care, the events that feel most scary, painful, or stressful (like a shot or blood draw) are likely to be the most memorable. Children may have trouble complying with routines during doctor's visits or accepting medication when needed. Given that medical care is typically happening because it's required for the health and safety of your child, it can be even more challenging to deal with toddler pushback. In issues of medical care, it's often essential to firmly, and lovingly, hold limits and boundaries.

Child's Perspective and Challenges

Different medical situations raise different challenges. When a medical need arises out of illness, like a doctor's visit due to an ear infection, the illness itself creates limitations for the child due to pain and fatigue. Younger toddlers may have trouble communicating their discomfort or needs, which can contribute to irritability.

For both sick and well visits, toddlers may experience a sense of losing control, particularly when medical needs require active interventions by doctors or caregivers, despite the child's protests. There may be times when administration of a required medical procedure, like a vaccine or blood draw, necessitates that parents or care providers restrain the child. By proactively creating opportunities that provide toddlers with a sense of control, within the constraints set by caregivers or doctors, parents can help increase a child's sense of safety, connection, and likelihood of compliance. Similarly, since unfamiliar or unpredictable medical care can activate a toddler's distress and create greater challenges for the family, preparing ahead can help mitigate the impact.

Parent's Perspective and Needs

Whether addressing a minor illness, like a runny nose and low-grade fever, or a more chronic medical condition, caring for the medical needs of your child can be challenging. Since your child's health and well-being take priority, unexpected or frequent calls to address these needs can be disruptive to your work schedule and childcare plans, perhaps contributing to more financial strain, exhaustion, and stress.

This stress can take an emotional toll as you deal with issues like managing your child's discomfort and distress, receiving conflicting information from various sources, waiting on test results, coping with uncertainty about what results mean for your and your child's future, and processing your own feelings as a caregiver. You may feel overwhelmed and saddened by your child's distress or limitations, or you may be grieving the loss of the straightforward developmental trajectory you had envisioned for your child. Even a common diagnosis like a food allergy may require a high level of parental vigilance in school and social settings, and it's normal to feel sadness and grief when beginning to figure out and navigate this new reality.

Parental stress related to your child's medical needs can understandably rattle your stance as a calm, steady leader to support and soothe your child. When this happens, it's important to lean on your coping strategies and social supports to care for your self-regulatory needs.

Practical Strategies to Try

- **Prepare ahead and talk about what to expect.** Kids are more likely to feel anxious if they don't know what to expect, or if they don't understand the rationale behind doctor's visits or medicine requirements. Using child-friendly, fact-based, and positively stated language, talk to your child about what they can expect and why ("This medicine is to keep your body healthy and strong," "The doctor is going to measure you on the scale to see how big you are growing"). Prepare your child similarly for potentially uncomfortable experiences, like getting a shot, with a realistic acknowledgment of discomfort and the short-term nature of pain, and a coping plan ("The doctor will give you a vaccine in your arm right here. It's medicine to keep your body healthy. It might feel like a little pinch, and then it will be over so fast. We can look at pictures or read a book to keep calm"). If you're not sure if the medical visit will include vaccines or blood draws, and you know your child fears these situations, call ahead to ask.
- **Find child-friendly resources.** There are many resources online to help families prepare for medical visits, procedures, or medications. Children connect well with visual tools and stories. Many TV shows, like *Sesame Street* and *Daniel Tiger's Neighborhood*, have episodes on YouTube about characters going to the doctor, taking medicine, or preparing to cope with routine medical procedures. Social stories are also a helpful tool that uses simple stories to tell kids what to expect and how to cope with tricky situations. Look up social stories related to the particular visit, procedure, or medical need you're addressing. Also, some hospitals and medical practices have child life specialists who provide child-friendly materials and support to help children and their families prepare and cope with different types of medical procedures. If you can't find what you're looking for online, create your own social story, including

the events to expect, feelings that might arise, and coping skills your child can use.

- **Invite your child to bring a comfort object, like a doll, stuffed animal, or favorite book.** Comfort objects can help children soothe and regulate when distressed and can provide a distraction or entertainment while sitting in the waiting room. Stuffed animals and dolls can also be used to help your child practice. If you're giving your child medicine in a syringe, allow them to build a sense of control and comfort by practicing administering "medicine" to their doll first.
- **Engage or distract.** Focusing attention away from pain or discomfort can help reduce the intensity of your child's discomfort. You might engage their attention in a related task, like encouraging them to watch the numbers change on the machine while getting their blood pressure taken. Some kids might respond better to an unrelated distraction, like listening to a story, watching a video, or playing a game like I Spy to notice objects around the room.
- **Validate, co-regulate, reward.** When your child is dealing with a painful or uncomfortable experience, validate their experience of pain and indicate that it's temporary ("Ouch, that shot felt like a pinch! It's over so fast!"). Co-regulate if needed (see "How to Soothe and Support," page 87). And celebrate success! Praise your child's bravery and their ability to do something hard, even if they had a meltdown. Consider motivating with a tangible reward, like a sticker, special toy, or TV time at home. Use the "first-then" formula to set the expectation ("First, we will get the X-ray to see a picture of your bones. Then we'll go to the bakery to get a cookie").

Other Common Struggles

My toddler has meltdowns every time we go to the doctor. What can I do?

Meltdowns in response to medical care come from a place of fear—fear of pain or the unknown. Some kids are more prone than others to anxiety related to medical care. You know your kid best. Adjust your expectations accordingly. The practical tools may not completely eliminate the meltdown, but if you can reduce the duration or intensity of the meltdown, consider that a win. Prepare your child in advance, as it helps them know what to expect and prepare for coping. Depending on the age, stage, temperament, and developmental needs of your child, you might want to prepare a few days earlier. Plan ahead for your own coping needs, too, to keep yourself as regulated as possible. Consider all stages: For example, do you anticipate a battle getting into the car seat before the appointment? If so, how can you motivate and calm your child? What choices can you offer to give them a sense of control (choosing the music in the car, choosing what toys to bring in a calming bag, etc.)?

As the authoritative parent, especially when it comes to mandatory health-care needs, it is essential to maintain your firm boundaries, despite the meltdown. This may mean physically holding down your child to make sure they get the care they need. As a parent, this is incredibly hard—both physically and emotionally! Regulate yourself and express empathy and compassion toward your child while firmly holding the boundary that this is necessary for their health. Seek support from available medical providers as needed.

My child is refusing prescribed medication. What should I do?

Sometimes, medication refusal is related to feeling out of control. Find opportunities for your child to feel a sense of control. That might look like offering them a choice between drinking the medicine from a syringe or cup, perhaps allowing them to hold the syringe and place it in their own mouth, or offering them two choices for a drink after the medicine to wash it down. Medication refusal might also just be because the medicine tastes bad. Ask your pharmacist whether an alternate, more palatable form of the medication is available, like chewable tablets or different flavor options.

Some parents surreptitiously mix medications into food to make it easier for their toddler to take. This strategy can be tricky because kids may detect the taste change, which then makes them avoid that food in the future *and* feel a sense of distrust toward the adult. It's also hard to measure whether they are consuming the full dose, and if they refuse the food, you've lost a dose. If this is a pathway you're considering, consult with your pediatrician to make sure it's acceptable to mix this particular medication. Then talk to your child openly about mixing the medicine with food ("I see it's hard to drink this medicine. Let's make it easier to swallow. Do you want to mix it with applesauce or yogurt?").

To encourage compliance with a daily medication, such as antibiotics, consider using a sticker chart, where your child earns a sticker for each day taking the medication and can redeem the stickers for a prize at the end of the week. Always remember the power of praise, and celebrate success!

Useful Reminders and Reframes

The following reminders and reframes can help encourage parents who are concerned by their toddler's struggles.

- It's hard to see my child suffer and struggle, and I'm doing my best to give them the best care they need.
- I feel stressed because I care deeply about my child's health and well-being.
- Pain and discomfort will fade. We can cope with this.

Pacifiers and Comfort Objects

A Practical Overview

Toddlers commonly rely on objects, such as stuffed animals, blankies, and pacifiers, as sources of comfort. During moments of separation from a loving caregiver, such as at bedtime, a comfort object can serve as a support to help them cope and self-regulate. Comfort objects can soothe anxiety around transitions, especially big changes, like starting a new childcare or welcoming a new sibling home. The use of pacifiers, bottles, and thumb-sucking are normal methods of toddler self-soothing, developed from the instinctive sucking reflex from infancy.

Sometimes, however, a child's use of a comfort object conflicts with parent preferences or values. Pacifiers, bottles, and thumb-sucking may be discouraged by pediatricians or dentists due to the impact on oral-motor or palate development. Although some parents feel concerned by their toddler's pacifier use or thumb-sucking, these oral self-soothing tools are unlikely to continue beyond early childhood for most. Yet, there may come a time when you choose to take a more proactive approach to reducing your toddler's use of comfort objects. As an authoritative parent, you can apply your balance of loving, supportive presence with the boundaries and limits you want to hold to provide consistent comfort within the necessary constraints of your toddler's developmental and environmental needs.

Child's Perspective and Challenges

As toddlers learn to navigate the world and cope with their feelings and experiences, they find comfort in familiar objects that represent a sense of safety and security, whether it's the cozy wrap of a worn blanket or the familiar sucking of a pacifier. Particularly in moments of heightened stress or transition, toddlers will seek out their comfort tool. This is a tremendous strength! As you're working so hard to help your child learn to self-regulate, recognize that their use of comfort objects is an age-appropriate self-regulatory skill.

Although it takes a different form, adults use comfort objects, too: Maybe it's a family photo on your desk that makes you smile when you're having a tough work day, or a favorite, lucky jacket that you wear to every sports event you attend. Consider how you'd feel if someone abruptly told you that you couldn't have these things anymore. Tune in to those feelings of disappointment, stress, or confusion as you approach making a change around your toddler's comfort objects.

Parent's Perspective and Needs

Although you can understand your child's reliance on their comfort objects, sometimes the demands of daily life make the use of these objects more challenging. You may feel concerned about the physical impact of pacifiers or thumb-sucking, or the hygiene of using these materials (yes, overused pacifiers can get pretty gross). You might be annoyed by the inconvenience of never being able to leave the house without your child's beloved stuffie. You may wonder if your child is "too old" to be carrying around a doll or blankie and feel concerned about the social implications, such as if your child might be teased by others. You might even feel pressured by friends or family to transition your child away from comfort objects like pacifiers.

Some parents feel daunted by the challenge of changing rules or limits around using comfort objects, while other parents may feel so sure about the change that they downplay the impact on their child. Remember your child's perspective and meet them where they are, so you can lovingly approach change with empathy and self-assuredness. Consider the rationale for making the change, and whether the benefits of removing the comfort object outweigh the potential costs.

Practical Strategies to Try

- **Plan alternatives for coping and self-soothing.** Comfort objects serve a powerful and necessary purpose for a toddler's self-regulation. If you'll be changing your child's access to his comfort object—whether that means removing a pacifier entirely or limiting it to bedtime only—consider what calming objects or tools they can use instead. You might find or buy a replacement comfort toy. Some children are soothed by using existing comfort objects in new ways. For example, talk to your child about how they can notice when they miss their pacifier and cuddle with their blanket instead, or ask you for a hug.
- **Talk about the change before it happens.** As with any big change, kids do best when they know what to expect. If you're planning to take their pacifier, talk about saying "bye-bye" to the pacifier several days before you plan to make the change. Explain the rationale for the change in developmentally appropriate, matter-of-fact language ("I know you love your pacifier. Your dentist says you need to stop using a pacifier because your mouth needs more space to grow. Let's figure out some other ways to help you feel cozy"). Avoid shaming language like "Only babies use pacifiers. You're not a baby, are you?" Use the countdown tools on page 138 to create a visual, concrete reminder of when the change will happen.
- **Include your child in a goodbye ritual.** This ceremony could be based in playful fantasy (for example, putting pacifiers in an envelope for the Pacifier Fairy, who will replace them with a different toy or comfort object) or based in honesty (such as creating a goodbye ceremony or song as your child places the pacifiers in the trash, or having your child give the pacifiers to their dentist, who has told them that their mouth needs more space to grow).

- **When it's time to make the change, completely get rid of all pacifiers**, for your sake and your child's. Yes, you might experience an extinction burst (page 73). Removing everyone's access to the pacifier will help protect you from the temptation to give in to their protests. With the proper planning in place, your child (and you) will quickly be able to use alternative coping tools instead. Provide big praise and celebration when your child is able to participate in the plan!
- **Consider the environment.** Some transitions in comfort objects may be limited only to certain situations, environments, or times of day. Maybe you want to ease into pacifier removal by limiting pacifier use to sleep time only, rather than all-day access. Use the strategies in this section to help your child prepare for the change, and set concrete rules around spaces—for example, pacifiers or blankies are only for sleeping or your bedroom. Encourage and allow access to the comfort object within those limits. For example, let's say your child has been carrying their blankie around all day and you're changing the routine to limit the blankie to the bedroom only. When they request their blankie during the day, you can encourage them to take a quiet moment in their bedroom with the blankie, allowing them access within the boundaries you set. Help plan for time and space transitions by acknowledging that the comfort object is a source of security and attachment. If the blankie is now limited to the bedroom, help your child say, "Bye-bye, blankie! Wait right here. I'll be back for naptime!" to help them more easily separate from the comfort object while supporting the idea of reconnection through a reunion plan.

Other Common Struggles

My toddler only wants to drink from a bottle. It soothes him, but he won't use a cup. What can I do?

Some children find comfort in their baby bottles. To them, a bottle represents much more than physical nourishment; it's a familiar source of comfort, security, and soothing. You may feel conflicted by your toddler's emotional connection to the bottle and/or their pediatrician's guidance to transition from baby bottles to toddler cups or to reduce milk intake to increase nutritional intake from other food sources. Parental pressure to eliminate the bottle can increase toddler and family stress, making your toddler's need to soothe with a comfort object even greater. Consider the cost-benefit trade-offs of eliminating bottle use. You might consider reducing bottle use to certain environments or times of day, while building up your child's toolbox of alternate self-soothing tools. Ultimately, he will eventually transition away from the bottle. Decide for yourself (and in consultation with your pediatrician, if needed) if this is a battle worth fighting. In either case, build up his connection reserves and support the development of a broader range of self-soothing tools.

How do I stop my toddler from thumb-sucking?

Unlike pacifiers, which parents can just throw in the trash, thumb-sucking can be much trickier to control. Most kids who suck their thumbs stop doing so on their own by age three, when they are better able to comprehend why thumb-sucking is a problem. Help your child figure out what they can do instead. First, try to identify the function of the behavior. If your child expresses that they like how their thumb feels in their mouth, help them replace thumb-sucking with a different oral-focused soothing behavior, like chewing on a chewable necklace or pressing their tongue to the roof of their mouth. If the enjoyment comes from the sensation in their hand, offer a squeezy stress ball as an alternative, or teach them to tense and relax their hand muscles by pretending to squeeze a lemon in their fist to make lemon juice, and then release.

Our child's daycare won't let her bring her stuffie from home. She carries it everywhere. What can we do?

Try to understand the rationale behind this rule and see if you can find common ground that meets everyone's needs. You may think your child will benefit from bringing their stuffie to daycare to help with separation anxiety, but the daycare doesn't want home toys to get lost or mixed in with other children's materials. Is there a limited time or place your child can use her stuffie at daycare for self-regulation, and then put the toy back in her bag? Otherwise, try to find other ways to help your child stay connected to their comfort object from a distance, like keeping a picture of the object at daycare, or (if they'll allow it), cutting a string from the stuffie or blanket and making it into a bracelet they can wear at school.

Useful Reminders and Reframes

The following reminders and reframes can help encourage parents who are concerned by their toddler's struggles.

- I want my child to have tools to calm and soothe themselves, and I can be resourceful.
- I can feel comforted that my child has an object they use as a source of comfort.
- I can help them find comfort and connection from other sources, too.

Starting New Childcare

A Practical Overview

Transitioning into a new childcare arrangement can bring up complex emotions and logistics for children and families. Whether your child is entering a childcare setting for the first time or transitioning from one childcare environment to another, it's a big change.

Identifying a new childcare placement can be a complicated process for families, as parents navigate the options, financial costs, schedules, commute, and teaching philosophy. Every family's needs and priorities are different. Community availability or financial constraints may limit your options, and you may need to choose something that doesn't check all your boxes. Choosing where to compromise can add stress to the transition plan.

When preparing to start new childcare, it can help to remember the core principles of authoritative parenting: leading with warmth while holding firm boundaries. It's absolutely normal for kids to express distress at first, which of course can be hard to witness and even make you question if you're making the right choice. These feelings are normal for everyone. With repetition of the separation and reunion process, children learn that (1) you will always come back for them, and (2) their big feelings are temporary and they can learn to cope.

Relationships are at the core of childcare transitions, so just remember this: In addition to strengthening the sense of security in the parent-child relationship through the separation and reunion process, your child will build new relationships with other caring adults and develop social relationships with peers that will enrich their development.

Child's Perspective and Challenges

As with any big change, toddlers feel challenged by the unfamiliar settings, people, and routines of new childcare. Uncertainty activates anxiety; conversely, kids benefit from knowing what to expect about the change. Separation fears are also very normal in toddlers; crying at drop-off is to be expected. For first childcare separation experiences, children may worry about whether their primary caregiver will come back, or if they did something wrong to scare their loved one off.

On the flip side, with this big change comes a lot of exciting opportunities. Some children may step into their new environment tentatively at first, whereas others may explore with boundless curiosity. They also have an opportunity to build a new relationship with another nurturing adult. Just as the primary caregiver serves as a secure base from which children feel safe to explore, the relationship toddlers build with their childcare providers ideally enriches their development and helps build trust in others.

A busy day in childcare, particularly when adjusting to a new setting, can be exhausting. Your toddler is very likely to be worn out and may melt down by pickup time after an active day of learning, exploring, and working hard to self-regulate through a new experience.

Parent's Perspective and Needs

When choosing a new childcare situation, you'll need to juggle many elements that inform decision-making: the expense, logistical issues, aligning philosophies with providers (for example, level of structure, time outdoors, play opportunities, response to challenging behaviors), and many others.

Parents may experience social pressures to approach childcare planning in a certain way, be it extended family members opining on how long a primary caregiver should stay home with their toddler, or friends debating the merits of center-based versus home-based care.

If you're feeling judged or inundated by unhelpful opinions, do your best to tune them out, and hold on to the input that best aligns with your family's needs.

Many feelings arise for parents around this transition, ranging from sadness about giving up time with your toddler to excitement at having some time to care for parts of your identity outside your parenting role (and for some, an added sense of guilt or self-judgment for looking forward to time away from your kid). These feelings are normal and valid. This transition is big for everyone, and over time, everyone will adjust.

Practical Strategies to Try

- **Talk about the change before it happens.** As with any big change, kids do best when they know what to expect. When possible, increase familiarity by visiting the new setting in advance or showing pictures of the new space and caregivers. With preparation and repetition, children will come to feel settled and secure in their new routines (see "Big Changes at Home," page 136, for additional tips).
- **Name and practice the plans for separating and reuniting.** Talk about the boundaries of drop-off and pickup in an honest, calm, and loving way. Explain the separation by telling the story about saying goodbye at drop-off and reuniting at the end of the day. Explain that you'll drop your child off with their caregiver and say, "Goodbye, Daddy loves you. Daddy always comes back. After rest time, you'll have a little extra playtime and then I'll pick you up." Address separation fears by acknowledging that you and your toddler are connected even when you're apart ("I will miss you when I am at work," "I'm excited to see you when I pick you up," and/or "I will always come back").

- **When dropping off at a new childcare setting, don't prolong your exit.** Crying at drop-off is normal, and some toddlers will try any trick they can think of to prevent you from leaving (even if you've talked about the change and practiced it repeatedly!), making it hard for parents to hold the boundary. Although our protective parental instinct may tell us to offer extra soothing, holding the boundary with a quick, loving goodbye and following through with the separation plan communicates your trust in your child's ability to cope and commitment to returning. Staying longer than the planned goodbye can create confusion for toddlers by mixing the message of "I really need to leave" with actually staying and reinforcing the child's protestations, inadvertently communicating a lack of confidence in the child to cope with the separation.
- **Avoid sneaking out or dishonesty.** Saying "I'm just going to get something from the car and I'll be right back," with no intention of returning until the end of the day might keep a child's meltdown momentarily at bay; however, doing so creates a sense of uncertainty about whether their adults are being honest.
- **Connect through a comfort object.** A transitional object from home, such as a small comfort toy, matching bracelets, or a family picture, can serve as a material reminder of your toddler's connection to you when you are apart. Give the comfort object an extra hug at the beginning of the day and remind your child that when they miss you, they can hug the object to feel the hug from you. You can reciprocate by talking about what you'll do when you miss them at work (like look at a picture or touch your matching bracelet).
- **Practice through games and role-play.** Role-play the goodbye plan at home with dolls or stuffed animals. You can also playfully practice communicating the message that parents always come

back through games like Hide and Seek, helping your child gain familiarity with the process of separation and reunion.

- **Unleash the power of praise.** Always remember to celebrate the success, or the steps toward success, of your child coping with the transition. In practice games at home, when your child engages in discussions about the plans, or when the actual event happens, use enthusiastic praise to highlight how well they are practicing, planning, and coping ("I loved giving you a hug when you found me in Hide and Seek!" "Great job practicing snuggling your stuffie when you miss me at school!").

Other Common Struggles

I disagree with how our child's care providers are handling certain situations. What should I do?

Parents and care providers may have conflicting attitudes toward naps, toilet training, bottle use, discipline, and approaches to play and learning. Sometimes the differing viewpoints are due to limitations within a childcare setting (for example, daycare can't follow the same nap routines as home due to the demands of keeping multiple children on the same schedule). Conflicting views can create tension between parent and childcare provider, raising questions about who knows best—is it the early childhood educator with a range of experience with many kids, or the parent who knows the ins and outs of their child's unique temperament, preferences, and moods better than anyone? The best approach is to aim for mutual respect. Try to maintain an open line of communication, with efforts to share openly and honestly with one another as you partner in your shared goals of providing loving, enriching care for your child.

Keep in mind that it's okay, even beneficial at times, for your child to be exposed to different caregiving approaches. However, if you recognize that the different approach is causing or may cause harm, take a more proactive role in discussing the concerns with the care providers. Always intervene when safety is a concern, or if problematic behaviors are being handled inappropriately and creating problems across settings. Before you do, take some time to cool down, and consider how you want to approach a conversation thoughtfully and collaboratively. You can review the tips in "When Caregivers Disagree," page 25, which can be applied to different types of relationships. Approach the conversation with curiosity, and try to limit assumptions. Work toward solving the identified problem, giving voice to both perspectives and avoiding blame.

My toddler melts down every morning when it's time to leave the house for daycare. What can I do?

You may have prepared for a few days of separation struggles at the start of new childcare, but the persistence of daily meltdowns is unexpected and unsustainable. As parents, it's painful to see our children struggling, and it's particularly stressful when you're trying to get into a stable rhythm and routine. As hard as it may be, continue to lovingly (maybe through gritted teeth and after a few deep breaths) hold the boundary that your child's job is to go to daycare and your job is to go to work. If the daily meltdowns continue, try to understand the "why." Does your child generally take more time than others to adapt to new environments? Are they expressing a dislike of daycare while at home, or only when it's time to separate? What do the care providers tell you about what's happening during the day? Might something be happening at school that's making your child feel unsafe or insecure, or are they generally happy once they get past the initial separation distress? If you can identify the "why," or at least narrow down the possibilities, you can take different approaches to try to ease the situation in partnership with the childcare providers, who may have added insight to offer.

My toddler seems to prefer being with their childcare provider instead of me. I should be happy that they have such a great caregiver, so why am I feeling so sad?

When children show preference for other caregivers over the primary parent, it can bring up a lot of complicated emotions for the parent, like sadness, jealousy, and guilt. All these feelings are totally normal. More often, though, the reality is less black and white. First, ask yourself what it is about your interactions with your child that give that impression. Is it that he whines when you pick him up or shows indifference? Clings to the care provider? Seems to behave better with them than with you? Before concluding that your child prefers you less, ask yourself, *Why else might he be reacting this way?* Difficulty transitioning away from the childcare provider at the day's end, for example, likely has more to do with the typical toddler tendency to struggle with transitions. It's also common for kids to behave differently with different caregivers, especially depending on the time of day. If your child is in full-time daycare, your primary time with them is during the hustle of the morning rush and the chaos of dinner and bedtime routines, both of which are often loaded with the tensions of hunger, fatigue, and time pressure—the perfect storm for a toddler meltdown and parental exhaustion.

Ultimately, as the primary caregiver, you will always be your child's number one. Having a childcare provider who your child loves is a gift, and does not take the place of the powerful love and connection between you and your child.

Useful Reminders and Reframes

The following reminders and reframes can help encourage parents who are concerned by their toddler's struggles.

- Goodbyes may be hard, but I trust that my child and I will be able to cope, and it will feel easier with time and practice.
- It's a gift for my child to feel connected to multiple caregivers and to be exposed to new social environments and different ways of caregiving.
- Time apart is time for me and my child to grow as individuals. I need to tend to other parts of my identity, just as my toddler will blossom through exposure to new experiences and relationships. They will feel my love during the time we have together, and we can feel connected even when we're apart.

New Baby and Siblings

A Practical Overview

Welcoming a new baby into the family can be an exciting and challenging time for families. There are practical changes in the household, like disruptions to daily routine, financial costs of a new baby and baby items, and the impact of a new baby's presence on space constraints in the home. Changes in the family dynamic will also occur. Conversations may be heavily focused on the baby and their needs, attention is divided between caring for both the toddler and the new child, parents are exhausted by the sleeplessness of caring for a newborn, and birthing parents are physically and emotionally recovering. Visitors may show a lot of excitement toward the new baby while paying less attention to the toddler.

It's clear how all these changes can impact your toddler and older children, even if your child is expressing excitement about the new baby. This section offers strategies for preparing parents and toddlers in advance. While many issues can be anticipated and proactively addressed, others may be difficult to plan ahead for or entirely unexpected. Address anticipated changes and needs to the best of your ability, while also recognizing limits and allowing yourself grace and flexibility.

Child's Perspective and Challenges

When anticipating the arrival of a new sibling, toddlers are likely to experience mixed feelings, some of which may be hard to name. They may feel excited and eager to meet their new playmate, and then later have difficulty understanding how boring and fragile newborns are. If a toddler witnesses everyone around them expressing excitement for the new baby, they may feel like they can only show positive feelings, hiding other feelings, like worries about the changes. As toddlers process their emotions internally, they may express them through challenging behaviors, which may be directed toward the new sibling, parents, or seemingly unrelated contexts as they seek to establish a sense of control. Toddlers may also not fully understand the permanence of the new family member, and it's common for toddlers to either verbally express or behaviorally act in a way that communicates that they have had enough of the baby and want life to go back to how it was.

Toddlers may view parental attention and affection as a limited resource that they struggle to share with the addition of a new sibling, particularly if they were previously an only child. Kids might feel a sense of being replaced as they observe so much attention being showered on the new baby. They may show more baby behaviors, like crying or expressing a desire for diapers, pacifiers, or bottles, because they've seen the baby get adult attention this way.

Toddlers may also feel confused or overwhelmed by their new role. When your child hears everyone talking to him about "being a big brother," he might be trying to make sense of this new identity: *What does that mean for me and who I am? Who will take care of me now?* Parents can validate the duality of the new role, holding space for both the "big sibling" role and acknowledging that he will still be loved and taken care of ("You're a big brother, and you're still my baby").

Parent's Perspective and Needs

Preparing for the arrival of a new baby looks very different when you're already actively parenting a toddler! Parents may have a long list to prepare for the new baby but limited bandwidth, as attention is consumed by existing parenting responsibilities, on top of personal, relational, and work needs.

You may worry about the adjustment to having a new sibling at home, both for your own needs and your toddler's, wondering, *Will*

I have enough time and attention to focus on my toddler? Will I love the new baby as much? You might feel sad about the lack of individualized time with the new baby, in contrast to the one-on-one bonding time you had with your firstborn. Or, if you spend a lot of time with the baby, you might feel sad about how much time this takes away from you and your toddler.

When a new baby comes home, parents commonly struggle most with high-demand times for the baby, like feeding, soothing to sleep, and bathing. These challenges look different depending on the age gap between siblings. Parental bandwidth is even more limited with closer age gaps, when the older child is still highly dependent on the parents for getting their needs met.

Recognize that all these reactions and adjustments are common and temporary, albeit challenging. Adjust expectations for yourself and have confidence that, in the not-too-distant future, you will make it through the hardest part and have given both of your children the greatest gift—a sibling and lifelong friend.

Practical Strategies to Try

- **Talk about the change before it happens.** Although some parents may be eager to share news about a pregnancy with their toddler as soon as they learn about it, pregnancy is long and a toddler doesn't have a strong concept for the length of time. You might consider telling your toddler when they start to notice changes, such as the growth of a pregnant belly or preparation of a nursery. Try to find a concrete way to help your child understand the new baby concept and the timing, like "The baby will come in the fall when the leaves are falling off the trees" or "The baby will come after you turn three."
- **Emphasize the good and start preparing them for change.** When talking about the new baby, focus on the positive aspects

of what your toddler will gain, like "more love and fun for our family." Acknowledge facts about babies to prepare your toddler for changes in routines, like "New babies are boring at first. They mostly just eat and sleep until they get enough strength to learn how to play" and "Babies need a lot of extra help while they are learning and growing. They cry because they don't have words to tell us what they need." As you get closer to the due date, start discussing practical changes to your toddler's daily routines. You may need to let them know that sometimes your co-parent will be getting her up in the morning, or that they may need to be patient sometimes when they want something. Try to keep it positive ("Babies need a lot of extra help from grown-ups, and sometimes you may need to wait a bit. Let's think of some ideas to make waiting more fun!").

- **Normalize the range of mixed feelings toddlers may express.** In anticipation, and upon arrival, of the new baby, they may feel excited for a new sibling, jealous of the baby's attention from caregivers, and/or worried about being replaced. Flip back to "How to Soothe and Support," page 87, for tips on helping toddlers make sense of their emotions.
- **Acknowledge your own feelings about preparing for the change.** You may have other ideas of how you want to prepare. Some of these may relate to your toddler, like wanting them to be weaned off bottles, or potty trained, or transitioned into a big-kid bed. Adjust expectations for yourself. Consider whether accomplishing certain readiness tasks before baby's arrival is actually as necessary as you feel. Ask yourself, *Does this really need to be on my plate? Can I delegate it, postpone it, or let it go?*
- **Set aside special one-on-one time with your toddler.** When welcoming a new baby at home, toddlers will crave individualized parent attention even more than usual. Review "Fill Your Connection Reserves," page 53, for reminders on how to

implement a daily routine of high-quality, child-led playtime. Remember, even just five minutes of high-quality, child-directed play can fill up your toddler's need for connection and will reduce their efforts to seek your attention through more problematic behaviors. Making space for daily individualized playtime with your toddler also communicates that baby doesn't always get priority attention.

- **Avoid blaming the baby.** Toddlers are prone to feel jealous about the frequent and immediate attention often given to babies, whose needs may be more urgent. To prevent a buildup of feelings of jealousy and resentment, avoid blaming the baby when explaining to your toddler why you're not available, and help your child find ways to make waiting easier. If your toddler asks you to play together, instead of saying, "I can't play with you right now. I need to get the baby to sleep," try saying, "I would love to play with you! I'll be ready soon. Do you want to eat a snack or play with your dolls while you wait for me?"

Other Common Struggles

How do I navigate the demands of parenting a toddler while managing the fatigue/nausea/discomfort of pregnancy?

Parenting a toddler is exhausting. And how much more so when doing it while pregnant! There's the added level of fatigue that pregnancy brings, physical symptoms like nausea, limited mobility of a growing belly—the list goes on. It's okay—and often necessary—to adjust your expectations for yourself. Though you may not be as active with your toddler as you want to be, you will make it through. Offer simple explanations to your toddler while managing their expectations. For example, in response to your toddler's request for your involvement in active play, explain, "My body needs to rest" and offer alternatives for what you can do together, like read a book on the couch or play

Guess the Animal, where your toddler can actively pretend to be an animal while you restfully guess while lying down. Give yourself grace. Though it may feel endless when you're in it, this stage is temporary.

Our toddler is having behavioral regressions, acting out in school and behaving aggressively. What can we do?

Toddler behavioral changes and regressions are more common than not when adapting to the changes associated with a new baby at home. Sometimes these behavior changes happen shortly after the new baby comes home; other times, they pop up months later as the reality of the new normal sets in.

Common challenging behaviors associated with a new sibling at home might include an increase in aggressive or oppositional behaviors, disruptions to sleep habits, potty-training regressions like increased accidents, or even asking for a bottle or to nurse. Some behavioral changes are related to the toddler seeing how much attention and care the baby gets, so they start acting in ways to get attention like the baby. Your toddler might notice that you go to the baby right away when the baby cries, so they start crying more. Challenging behaviors may be directed toward the baby, like hitting or grabbing toys. Other times, toddlers may treat their baby sibling with excess kindness and sweetness, but direct behavioral outbursts toward parents or in other situations.

Recognize that these challenging behaviors are not due to malicious intent, but more often out of the toddler's need to feel connected. Instead of focusing on shaming or punishing your toddler for challenging behaviors, focus on meeting their needs through increased connection. Try to prioritize daily special one-on-one time with your toddler to proactively address their need to connect with you. For additional strategies to address challenging behaviors, refer to "Learn to Influence Young Children's Behavior," page 61. Use selective attention to give more focus on positive behaviors and underreact or ignore minor misbehaviors. Make an effort to catch your child doing the positive opposite of the problem behavior (for example, instead of grabbing a toy from the baby, they make an effort to take turns), and provide enthusiastic praise, allowing them to feel connected and capable and shifting the attention toward positive rather than problematic behaviors.

It's also okay to play along to a degree with a toddler's attempts to act like a baby, like wanting to be carried or rocked. As your toddler navigates their new identity as a big sibling, momentarily playing along with their baby-like urges can soothe them while also providing the reassuring comfort that you continue to love and care for them and they are not being replaced.

What can I do about feelings of heightened anxiety, depression, or other mental health concerns?

It's common for caregivers to experience increased stress following the birth of a new baby (even when not the first baby). Both birthing and non-birthing parents can experience "baby blues," with feelings of sadness or irritability. Baby blues tend to stabilize after the first few weeks, but when these feelings persist, this can be a sign of postpartum mood or anxiety disorders, including post-traumatic stress disorder following a traumatic birth. Such issues are common, yet many new parents go undiagnosed and untreated. Please don't allow mental health concerns to burden you—help is available and there are many effective treatments. You deserve to take care of yourself and enjoy this time with your new baby. Strategies specific to the postpartum period are beyond the scope of this book, but there are many incredible postpartum resources that can support you. Share concerns about your mood and well-being with your therapist, primary doctor, child's pediatrician, or your OB-GYN. Postpartum Support International (postpartum.net) is a wonderful organization that provides a helpline for struggling parents to call (1-800-944-4773), as well as resources on local and national levels.

Useful Reminders and Reframes

The following reminders and reframes can help encourage parents who are concerned by their toddler's struggles.

- My love for my children is not finite; it will continue to expand and grow for each additional child.
- Change is hard for everyone, and it's temporary. We can cope. And in the long run, having a sibling will be a lifelong gift for our toddler (and vice versa).
- When considering how to prioritize my time, I can ask myself, *Is this really a need? Or is it a wish that I can let go?*

Dealing with Fear and Anxiety

A Practical Overview

Anxiety is a normal human experience. It can be a helpful and adaptive function to alert us to threats in the environment. If the smoke detector goes off in your house, it can be lifesaving to feel worried, motivating you to jump into action quickly and ensure everyone's safety. But sometimes that smoke detector goes off because you forgot to set a cooking timer and your roasted broccoli is burnt. There's no real dangerous situation, but the alarm has been set off. Compare that to internal signals: Anxiety becomes more of a problem when your bodily smoke detector goes off unnecessarily, sending a signal that a situation is threatening, even when it's actually a neutral, safe situation (like giving a presentation to a group at work, or a toddler going to a friend's house for a playdate for the first time).

Toddlers and young children commonly feel afraid of the unfamiliar and unknown, whether it's new people, environments, or activities; loud, sudden sounds; or separation from a parent. As the imagination develops throughout the early childhood years, kids may become more fearful as they imagine a broader range of new situations, whether potentially realistic, like worry over losing a beloved stuffed animal, or complete fantasy, like fear of the dark because they imagine monsters hiding under their bed. When parents see their children struggling with fear and anxiety, a common, well-intentioned instinct is to swoop in to immediately alleviate the fear, perhaps by reassuring the child that monsters aren't real, or by staying in their room until they fall asleep to "protect" them from the imagined monsters (flip back to "Sleeping," page 107, for guidance on these kinds of fears).

Authoritative parents can help children learn to cope with anxiety by using a loving and supportive stance while holding appropriate boundaries that allow kids to build skills and confidence for coping with feared situations. This guide focuses on a general approach to navigating anxiety in young kids; however, see page 195 for additional resources on parenting anxious children. Some families benefit from a more individualized approach by working with a specialist.

Child's Perspective and Challenges

We know that toddlers express feelings through behaviors. When a young child feels anxious or afraid, they might express their distress by whining or crying, clinging to a caregiver, acting out, or asking the same question repeatedly for reassurance. Without the language to express and address their big feelings, toddlers need caregivers to model and label their emotional experiences to help them make sense of their distress, and seek comfort to reassure them of their safety.

Toddlers need practice learning to tolerate and cope with anxiety. If a child has a meltdown because they're afraid to go in a swimming pool for the first time, getting to the other side of that meltdown without avoiding the pool altogether will help the child learn to build a tolerance for their emotions and confidence in their ability to cope.

Parent's Perspective and Needs

It's hard to see our kids struggle. When they do, many well-intentioned parents instinctively want to swoop in and help, to protect their child from distress or solve the anxiety-inducing problem. Sometimes, this looks like reassurance ("You're fine. There's nothing to be scared of"), whereas other times, it looks like avoiding the feared situation ("You can come sleep in our room").

Although these approaches may alleviate the distress immediately, it can be counterproductive to parenting goals of supporting development of children's autonomy and confidence. These kinds of accommodations end up putting more work on us, as we now have to calculate how to encourage our child to push through after previously giving in, and struggle with our own inability to tolerate the discomfort of seeing our child feel this way. As parents, we face the challenge of having to determine when to encourage and push our kids to engage with something that may make them anxious, like playing with a new friend, and rethink how much hands-on support is really needed to facilitate their autonomy and development without overstepping.

All that said, there may be times when your child's emotional needs feel insurmountable, or when overstepping or alleviating a meltdown is what you, as the parent, need in the moment, even if that goes against your long-term parenting goals and values. There is a cost to this because it reinforces the behavior, but as long as you know this, it's okay to give in occasionally. It's "good enough" parenting. However, if you find that you're consistently stepping in to alleviate meltdowns and are struggling to ride it out, consider connecting with a child therapist who can help both you and your child cope with fears and anxieties.

Practical Strategies to Try

- **Implement daily special time and consistent routines.** Daily use of special time and consistent routines are great foundations for mitigating the effects of childhood anxiety. Chapter 3 also has many useful tools for navigating tricky toddler emotions, including fear and anxiety. Refer to that chapter for a refresher on important strategies for navigating toddler emotions, like modeling, labeling, and validating.
- **Consider the message behind your message.** In response to a child's fear, you may have the instinct to reassure your child: "You're fine, there's nothing to worry about. That dog isn't going to bite you." Although this comes from a place of encouragement and the parental wisdom of knowing that your child will be okay and unharmed in this situation, this type of comment actually

invalidates the child's experience of fear, which is very real to them—making them feel misunderstood and disconnected. Some parents may also respond to their child's anxiety by removing the fear-inducing hurdle to protect them from distress. For a child melting down because they're afraid to get in the swimming pool, you might just want to avoid or end the meltdown by leaving the pool area. Although avoiding the feared situation may alleviate the child's feeling of fear in the moment, doing so sends a message: "You're right. This situation is too scary and too hard for you."

- **Use supportive language.** Child psychologist Dr. Eli Lebowitz has developed a framework of supportive language that parents can use to more effectively respond to kids' expression of anxiety:

  Validate the feeling + express confidence = supportive statement

  For example: "I can see that this is hard for you" + "I know you can handle it" or "I know you're feeling really worried" + "You've been able to cope with this before, and I know you'll be able to again."

  Validation is key to ensuring that your child feels seen and connected. Even if you don't agree with the fear, you're acknowledging that the feeling is real to them. At the same time, you can also encourage your child to face their fears, despite the discomfort, by expressing confidence in their ability to cope with a tough situation. Note that you don't need to respond to every single expression of fear with a supportive statement. Over time, the messages that you accept their feelings and believe in them will generalize across different contexts.

- **Remember the power of praise!** Celebrate the small successes. Even if your child continues to cry as they sit at the top of the slide that they're nervous to try, underreact to the crying while enthusiastically celebrating their efforts. Of course, if the crying goes on too long and there's a growing line behind them, you can help them down while praising their courage to climb the ladder or slide down.

- **Encourage bravery.** Using supportive statements is a great way to encourage bravery. First, identify the "brave behavior" by thinking about the opposite of the anxious behavior—the more specific, the better. For a child afraid to swim in the pool, the opposite brave behavior might be going in the pool with a parent holding them. When encouraging bravery, set realistic expectations. Your child might not yet be ready to fully submerge in the pool; a first brave step might be standing next to the pool, or sitting on the sides and dipping toes in. Help your child learn to cope with anxiety by exposing them to the right amount of anxiety—push them a bit outside their comfort zone so they feel the anxiety followed by the confidence- and skill-boosting pride of tolerating it. Breaking the "brave goal" into smaller parts is also a helpful way for parents to follow through on holding boundaries to encourage bravery without giving in to your child's protests. Offer specific praise for their steps toward bravery, even if they do so with shouts and tears!
- **Use selective attention (page 68).** Give more attention to brave actions while underreacting to anxious behaviors. First, label and validate your child's emotion, helping them feel understood. Provide specific praise for brave behaviors or steps toward bravery, like "Great job walking toward the jungle gym!" and underreact to anxious behaviors, like whining, crying, and repeating questions. Over time, brave behaviors will increase while kids learn to cope with anxious behaviors.
- **Offer a superhero pep talk.** Help kids talk back to fear by using their playful imagination. This strategy works best for preschool-age children. In preparing to approach a potentially fearful situation, like a playdate at a new friend's house, or the first day of a new daycare, help your child identify a favorite character or superhero who is brave. Ask your child to get into character,

pretending to be his favorite superhero giving advice to encourage bravery in himself. Role-play how it might go.

- **Create a feeling recipe.** Anxiety becomes a problem when it takes over. It's helpful for kids to realize that (1) feelings, like fear, don't last forever, and (2) multiple feelings, even those that seem to be opposites, can happen at the same time. Practice making a "feeling recipe." When a child expresses a worry (either verbally or nonverbally), label or reflect the feeling ("You look worried"), and then ask them to consider how much worry they feel: A small scoop? A big scoop? Then encourage them to consider what other feelings, and how much, can be mixed into the bowl: A small scoop of excitement? A large scoop of bravery? Two scoops of pride or curiosity? ("You're meeting your new teacher today. Do you think there is a scoop of excitement?") Mix all the feelings together. The fear becomes smaller and loses power, making it easier for kids to lean on their other feelings, too.

Other Common Struggles

It's hard to watch my child struggle with anxiety. My own anxiety gets in the way. What can I do?

I hear you. It *is* hard. And you might not follow through with the fear-fighting path you hope to take 100 percent of the time. Give yourself some grace and recognize your own coping needs. When making a plan to address your child's fear, make a key part of that plan to strategize for your own emotion regulation (see "Self-Soothe and Self-Regulate," page 85). Identify a strong support person you can call when you need encouragement. Recognize your limits and offer yourself compassion. Take a break when needed. If your anxiety interferes with your ability to help your child be brave and do hard things, it can help to speak with a therapist to address your own needs. See page 195 for mental health resources.

My child's fears are getting in the way of our daily routines. She's afraid to stay home with a babysitter, sleep alone, and even get dropped off at school. How can we cope?

Beyond caring deeply for your children and wanting them to feel at ease, dealing with childhood anxiety can be particularly draining for parents, as it can demand much of your time and attention. Consider what else might be going on. Sometimes, parents get impatient or have set expectations too high (then we say, "Pull yourself together! This isn't such a big deal!"), which gets in the way of helping the child cope by invalidating their experiences. On the other end of the spectrum, especially when distress is high, parents are more likely to change their own behaviors and loosen boundaries to reduce the immediate distress and protect their child (and maybe their own schedules or sanity) from the discomfort of a fear-induced meltdown. This is referred to as an accommodation. For example, for a child afraid of the dark, an accommodation might be lying next to your child until they fall asleep, or for a child who is worried around strangers, an accommodation might be parents never leaving the child with a sitter, at the expense of their own needs and schedules. Dr. Eli Lebowitz's book, *Breaking Free of Child Anxiety and OCD*, explores how to reduce accommodations to help address child anxiety problems. It can also be life-changing to seek out the support of a specialist to help navigate this process. See page 195 for resources.

How do I know if my child's behavior is driven by anxiety or something else?

Many people view anxiety as an internal problem. However, children can also express anxiety through irritable moods and aggressive behaviors, which may not look like your expected presentation of anxiety. Consider the context of the behaviors and ask yourself, *Why else might my child be acting this way?* Recall that some of these behaviors can be reactions to hunger, fatigue, or disconnection. We've also talked about common toddlerhood fears as they relate to anxiety.

Young children may also demonstrate anxiety when a task is beyond their ability level, or when unsure how to navigate a social interaction. They may express their fears with clear language, but more often with whining, clinginess, crying, shouting, throwing themselves on the floor, or aggressive behaviors toward others. Although most toddlers and preschoolers show some of these behaviors at times, parents may consider seeking out specialized support when these behaviors become so frequent or intense that they interfere with daily functions and routines.

Useful Reminders and Reframes

The following reminders and reframes can help encourage parents who are concerned by their toddler's struggles.

- My child is capable of trying hard things.
- If I show I believe my child can cope, they will gain confidence that they can cope.
- I can gain perspective by asking myself, *Is my worry about my child's suffering greater than their actual suffering?*

Risky Play Versus Unsafe Behaviors

A Practical Overview

Many parents of toddlers are especially sensitive to risk, having an instinctive, evolutionarily adaptive drive to protect their offspring from perceived threats and harm. Although culturally dependent, our modern life has fewer opportunities for kids to learn through risky play, with less time for unstructured play and time in nature, for example. Much of modern childhood is directed and controlled by adults. For these reasons, both parents and kids have less opportunity to build a tolerance for developmentally appropriate risk.

Yet, children instinctively are motivated to play in physically challenging ways, like climbing and wrestling, that risk-averse adults may view as concerning. Physical play is adaptive, helping kids develop strength, coordinate movements with motor planning, learn their own physical limits and boundaries, recognize the needs and boundaries of others, and develop confidence as they learn to tolerate fear and risks.

The authoritative parent aims to support the development of autonomy through warmth and appropriate limits. In the case of risky play, that actually means allowing kids to explore, take risks, and fail within appropriate constraints so they learn to problem-solve, build confidence, and gain physical and emotional strength. When caregivers jump in too soon, preventing a child from trying a physical challenge on their own, all these valuable learning pathways are disrupted.

There are times when "risky play" becomes a true unsafe behavior, when the strength and wisdom of a firm and caring adult is required. Yet the line between "risky play" and "unsafe behaviors" can be hard to identify. We'll explore this next.

Child's Perspective and Challenges

Kids' natural tendencies toward playfulness, curiosity, and boundary testing all contribute to risky play. For example, many kids are naturally drawn to *play* fight, with an intended emphasis on *play*. Physical play involves a great deal of imagination, and even play fighting (without physical harm) can be a creative, learning process for children. Risky play allows children to explore their interests while contributing to their physical development and coordination, ability to relate to others, respect of personal boundaries, and emerging confidence and sense of autonomy.

Often, risky or unsafe behaviors can be related to a toddler's natural instinct to test boundaries, whether they're looking to see how you react when they climb onto the kitchen table and prepare to jump off, or when they run beyond the boundaries of the playground fence (see "Decoding Difficult Behaviors," page 33).

When unsafe behaviors pose a true safety concern or come from a place of dysregulation or lack of control, children need their bigger, stronger, wiser parent to step in to protect, soothe, redirect, and hold boundaries.

Parent's Perspective and Needs

As parents, we want our children to explore and build independence, but often, our instinct to protect them from harm kicks in. It's evolutionarily adaptive to feel distress when we assess that our child (or any child!) is at risk. We may see a risky behavior that sets off our internal alarm bells, alerting us to react and intervene in a potentially dangerous situation. That quick, automatic intervention can be helpful for preventing harm in the moment, but as we look at the big picture around development of resilience and problem-solving skills, it's easy to see how our child will benefit when we develop strategies to effectively determine when to step in or hang back.

Supporting kids in risky play requires us to access our own self-awareness and emotion regulation skills, building our own tolerance for watching our kids struggle and fail. We also need to be aware of how our kid's risk tolerance may depend on personality characteristics and abilities, and to be aware of our own limits, such as a common first-time-parent tendency to be more protective of an oldest child.

Practical Strategies to Try

- **Set your intention and make a coping plan.** Make a plan for how you want to approach risky behaviors to support your child's development. Consider how your approach may be different depending on the situation, like in an environment that requires parent direction (like the grocery store) versus a free-play situation (like the playground).
    - Plan questions that you might be able to ask yourself in a moment of live assessment, such as:
        - Is there a developmental benefit to this type of play or behavior? Is this promoting their development of their motor skills and planning, confidence, peer relationships, creativity, or curiosity?
        - In reality, how risky is this situation?
        - Does the potential for harm outweigh the long-term benefits of allowing this type of play or behavior?
        - What level of risk am I able to cope with?
        - What could be the worst-case scenario here? How likely is that to happen?
    - Once you've identified your overall intention and assessment questions, make a coping plan for yourself. If you're choosing

to hang back while you allow your child to explore a potentially risky play situation:

- Take a deep breath (or three, or five) to help you cope with the discomfort by regulating your activated nervous system.
- Remind yourself of your overall parenting goals and the developmental benefits for your child with a mantra or words of encouragement for yourself, like *Mistakes are for learning; allowing them to fall helps them learn and grow; a little pain and discomfort is temporary.*
- Imagine how the exploratory play now can translate into a resilient, creative, curious problem solver in the future.
- Consider what you can say and do to supportively intervene when safety becomes a real issue so you feel prepared and more in control, even as you sit back.

- **Step back.** Support autonomy and facilitate independence by taking a step back from closely supervising play. Hovering too closely to your child when they are trying to explore a new environment or try out a tricky skill communicates that you don't trust their abilities, and they may learn to not trust themselves. Create opportunities for play situations where you can take a hands-off approach to supervision—watch from a distance without physically or verbally stepping in unless truly necessary. Accept that falls and bruises will happen, and bodies will heal.
- **Teach the skill.** Rather than intruding on exploratory play with "Be careful!" or "Don't do that!" help bring your child's attention to the environment to help them make their own judgments and mistakes. For example, if your child is climbing on a pile of rocks at the park, internally identify your fears and bring their attention to the aspects of the environment that you are noticing. You might say,

"Some rocks look slippery. Notice how your feet feel on the rocks to make sure you feel steady."

- **Teach your child to assess the environment.** This will help build their awareness, problem-solving, skills, and confidence. If your child is swinging a broom around because they're pretending to use it as a superhero prop, you may view this as unsafe, even though their intention is playful and imaginative. First, assess the risk. If unlikely to cause serious harm, let them play and learn. If they're getting close to damaging materials or hurting others, prompt them to look at the environment, and then establish the rules ("If you want to keep playing with your superhero wand, we need to make sure everyone else is safe"). Next, show them where there is a safe space to play that activity. In this way, you're allowing the child's autonomy, and rather than interfering, you're helping them learn the skills to assess themself in space.

Other Common Struggles

How do I teach my child to not cross the line between play fighting and real fighting?

Allowing play fighting encourages opportunities for kids to learn and problem-solve on their own. Yet, kids need parents to reinforce boundaries and limits (see "Set the Expectation," page 66). Depending on the age, stage, and abilities of the children involved in play fighting, adults will make different decisions about when to step in and when to allow children to try to resolve conflict on their own. Particularly in the early childhood years, when choosing to hang back to allow more child-directed peer play, it's still best to maintain a supervisory role so you can step in swiftly when needed.

When you need to intervene, view it as an opportunity to teach skills related to consent and social cues. You can prompt children to look at each other and ask, "How do you think she's feeling?" When kids can recognize that frowns or tears are nonverbal signs that the play is no longer fun, they'll learn to adjust those play behaviors in the future. You can also teach kids to say and respond to "Stop!" when the play fighting becomes too much. Praise them for using the skills ("Great job telling Joey that you are done playing this way") and for backing off when their playmate says stop ("Great job listening and respecting Juan's words and body").

How can I discourage my toddler's unsafe behaviors, like running off, in public places?

Handling unsafe behaviors in public can feel so overwhelming. You know your kid best. If you know they're prone to unsafe behaviors in public, like running into the street or running off at the grocery store, review "Learn to Influence Young Children's Behavior," page 61, to make a proactive plan for how you can prepare for predictably tough situations. Some particularly helpful tools include the liberal use of praising positive opposites (page 132) and establishing rules and expectations for how those rules will be enforced, with plans for consistent follow-through. Establishing a plan is key to calmly holding a boundary with authority; this way, you don't need to think on your feet in a moment of panic, and it sets up your child for success by making clear the plan in advance.

You might also consider your threshold for what classifies as unsafe behaviors. Consider the behavior and the environment. Running off toward a busy street is much riskier than running off within a fenced-in playground. Once you can reassess the actual risk, recalibrate your approach accordingly.

I want to let my kids play a bit more freely, but my own fears get in the way. What can I do?

First, acknowledge your bravery in recognizing this in yourself. This is a completely understandable experience. As parents, our job is to keep our kids safe and well. Your instinct to intervene when you witness potentially risky play comes from a place of deep love and care. You might recognize the competing urges you have to allow your child to play freely while also wanting to prevent any harm from befalling them. Use your own coping tools (see "Self-Soothe and Self-Regulate," page 85) as you learn to tolerate your child engaging in risky play. It's also perfectly reasonable to acknowledge your limits. If you recognize your instinct is to hover as your child navigates playground equipment, consider whether there is a co-parent or another caregiver who can be the primary playground supervisor.

Useful Reminders and Reframes

The following reminders and reframes can help encourage parents who are concerned by their toddler's struggles.

- I recall times when I have held back from stepping in, and my child was okay. Going forward, I can add these experiences to a growing mental data bank to help remember those wins in the future.
- I expect cuts and bruises; bodies are designed to heal.
- My job is to keep my children safe. I may feel afraid when I worry for their safety. What could be the worst-case scenario here? How likely is that to happen? What level of risk am I able to tolerate?

Discussing Hard Topics Like Death

A Practical Overview

Unfortunately, many families experience or witness challenging, traumatic, or stressful circumstances, such as deaths, community violence, homelessness, racism, or scary news events. Regardless of whether kids have direct exposure to these circumstances, they can pick up on the stress of their caregivers. Some adults may seek to protect their children from exposure to these stressors by entirely avoiding any hint of information about the situation, whereas other adults may seek transparency, wanting to find a way to share the difficult topic with their children. Parents may struggle to know how and when to talk to children about stressful or scary events.

Typically, some acknowledgment of the stressor is helpful for young children. Without any explanation offered, kids may feel confused about changes in their caregivers' affect, behaviors, or routines, and they may jump to their own conclusions about a worst-case scenario or innocently blame themselves for changes they experience. A basic explanation might be as simple as, "Daddy is feeling sad right now, so he needs to take a break from playing. He will feel better soon." Depending on the child's developmental level, they may have more questions, or parents may choose to share more information in alignment with family values. When a stressor impacts your child's daily routine in a concrete way (like the death of a family member, teacher, or friend), offer more information in a developmentally appropriate way.

Ultimately, every family and situation is different. You know your child best, and it's most important to meet them where they are. Adapt the following guidelines to your child's and family's needs, and integrate the guidance of your familial, cultural, or religious values wherever appropriate.

Child's Perspective and Challenges

When families or communities experience stressful events, kids pick up on the stress of their caregivers, whether or not the topic is explicitly discussed. Though their emotions may not be fully verbalized, young children's reactions can present in play themes, regressed behaviors, complaints of physical ailments, crying, changes in eating and sleeping habits, nightmares, or worries about the safety of others.

Kids have varying capacities to take in the details of a stressful event. Without clear answers to the questions they may have, kids will mentally "fill in the blanks" to try to make sense of the situation. They may worry that they are the cause of the harm. This is why when kids are curious, it's helpful to provide opportunities to ask questions.

Young children are concrete thinkers. When addressing a hard topic like the death of a loved one, kids may not understand the permanence of death. Caregivers might even hear questions like, "Will Grandma come to my birthday party?" both in the immediate aftermath and during future milestones.

Parent's Perspective and Needs

If you're reading this section, you might be experiencing a difficult or stressful situation that you want to broach thoughtfully with your children. If so, I want to acknowledge the tremendous strength it takes to proactively consider supporting your children through this when you are also trying to process your own emotions. What you're experiencing may require a lot of your attention, energy, and emotional bandwidth, and it's okay to recognize that your parenting battery may be lower for now. Take care of yourself first. Gather your social supports and resources to make sure your parenting battery is as full as it can be (and accept that it won't be fully charged).

Parents may have an expectation for how kids will respond to the difficult topic and then often end up being surprised by their kid's reaction, which may be simpler or more complex than anticipated.

Approach difficult conversations with a matter-of-fact, nonjudgmental, open-minded stance. Share some of your own feelings to model and normalize emotional expression during difficult times, but also recognize that your child may feel or express emotions differently.

Practical Strategies to Try

- **Maintain consistency and routines.** Whether or not you're dealing with practical changes in routine impacted by the difficult situation, remember that maintaining consistency and routines will provide a sense of comfort and security to your children, even if their information about the situation is limited. Parental stress can unintentionally spill over to kids, and doing your best to keep everyone grounded in the familiarity of routines will help reinforce a sense of safety and security for your child. In explicit conversations about difficult topics, you can talk to your child about what will change and what will stay the same so they know what to expect. That being said, there are certain situations, like a family death, where maintaining routines may be extraordinarily difficult in the immediate aftermath. Offer yourself compassion.
- **Be intentional with information.** Decide what information actually needs to be shared with your child and when it needs to happen. If the topic isn't necessary or urgent to discuss, you can delay talking about it, which gives you more time and space to process the situation and prepare yourself for supporting your child.
- **Keep talks simple.** When talking about difficult topics, share information in bite-sized pieces and developmentally appropriate language. Focus on facts and avoid euphemisms, which can create more confusion. If a caregiver explains death as "Mommy is sleeping," a child might then become afraid of sleeping. Use accurate language like, "Mommy died. Her heart stopped beating." Allow questions and keep your answers simple. You might choose to say

something simple around your faith if you practice, but recognize that as concrete thinkers, toddlers will likely take anything at face value, such as equating "Mommy's in a better place" with a place they can visit. Avoid elaborating too much, since kids have limited bandwidth and understanding to take in difficult topics. Follow your child's lead by offering additional information if they ask, and be open to more questions in the future. Avoid exposing kids to stressful adult conversations or scary media.

- **Expect the unexpected.** Kids' reactions to stressful events can vary. Some reactions may be immediate; others delayed. They may express their feelings through behavioral regressions, changes in sleeping and eating patterns, or in imaginative play themes. These are all normal responses to grief and stress and tend to improve within four to six months, though you can expect ongoing questions or reactions around anniversaries or milestone events. Your child may seem unfazed when you tell them Grandpa died, and then, months later, they may be inconsolably sad to realize that Grandpa won't be attending Grandparents' Day at school. Some parents may expect more emotional distress from their child than what's expressed. Try to relinquish any sense of expectation, and maintain your stance as a present, supportive, loving caregiver, regardless of how your child processes the information.
- **Find and use concrete tools.** Young kids are concrete thinkers. When the situation allows and your child's interests align, try to use concrete tools to respond to the situation. For example, if commemorating a loss, use physical mementos such as photos to help kids connect to goodbye rituals.
- **Stay connected.** Regardless of how your child responds to the difficult topic or stressful event, they will feel more secure when caregivers maintain daily routines of connection and positive attention. Incorporate a short, daily parent–child playtime (see "Fill Your Connection Reserves," page 53). It will help you as a parent

mindfully and playfully connect to your child when you might otherwise feel emotionally depleted or disconnected.

Other Common Struggles

My child is asking tough questions. How do I respond?

Even very young children can surprise us with their ideas or questions on hard topics that parents aren't sure how to answer. The question or idea may catch you off guard, you might be unsure of the right language to use, or perhaps you're not sure whether answering the question will help or harm your child's processing of the situation. It's okay to acknowledge that you're not sure or not ready to respond. Validate your child's feelings and curiosities, acknowledge your limits, and communicate connection with a supportive presence. For example, you might say, "I know you have a lot you're wondering about. I do, too. I'm not sure how to answer that yet. I'm here for you, and I love you." When you are ready to answer, do so with simple, fact-based responses, without offering more information than needed.

My co-parent and I have been separated for three months, and now suddenly, my toddler is acting up. Could there be a connection?

It's common for young children to experience changes in behavior in response to increased stressors, such as the prolonged absence of a caregiver. Sometimes the behavioral changes are immediate, whereas others might present as a more delayed response, such that parents may not immediately attribute the behavioral change to the stressor. Even though these behavioral changes can be extraordinarily difficult for caregivers to manage, they are normal and common responses to stress, and more often than not, temporary. Review "Decoding Difficult Behaviors," pages 33–43, for specific tips to address some common stress-response behavioral changes. Offer compassion to yourself and your child for the tough time you are both going through.

Continue filling up connection reserves (page 53). If possible, work together with your co-parent to maintain your balanced stance as loving, attuned caregivers, while also holding the boundaries your child needs.

I'm stressed and depleted. How can I support my toddler when my own tank is empty?

Recognize your limits and take care of yourself first. Review chapter 3 for strategies to help with your own self-regulation and stress management. Connect with your social support system, and ask for help in supporting your child, too. Do they have a favorite aunt or kind neighbor? If so, get them involved. Adjust your expectations for yourself, especially if your bandwidth is too limited to use most of the strategies discussed in this guide. That's okay. The intensity of toddler parenting stress decreases as your child grows. Work within your limits and lean on short periods of high-quality, tuned-in parent-child connection time to fill your reserves.

Useful Reminders and Reframes

The following reminders and reframes can help encourage parents who are concerned by their toddler's struggles.

- I can try my best to be a steady, loving presence for my child, even if my tank isn't full. I don't need to give 100 percent right now.
- My toddler is curious. I can be patient and truthful while respecting their innocence.
- This stressor is temporary, and the acute pain will fade over time. Likewise, regressions don't last forever, even if they feel that way.

RESOURCES

SOME HELPFUL BOOKS TO READ TO YOUR TODDLER

Learning About Feelings

In My Heart by Jo Witek (a book about feelings)

The Color Monster by Anna Llenas (a book about feelings)

My Feelings Are Waves by Nell Harris (a book about feelings)

Catching Thoughts by Bonnie Clark (a book about building emotion awareness)

Coping with Separation

The Invisible String by Patrice Karst (deals with separations, including daily separation anxiety and missing people who have died)

The Kissing Hand by Audrey Penn (a book about separation fears)

Someone to Be With by Deidre Quinlan

Preparing for a New Sibling

Hello in There! by Jo Witek

Big Brother Daniel by Angela C. Santomero

Getting Along with Friends

Llama Llama Time to Share by Anna Dewdney (a book about sharing and new friends)

Little Blue Truck by Alice Schertle

Mindfulness

Mindful Monkey, Happy Panda by Lauren Alderfer (a book for practicing mindfulness)

Persistence

Jabari Tries by Gaia Cornwall (a book about persistence)

Preparing for a Doctor's Appointment

Leo Gets a Checkup by Anna McQuinn

Franklin Goes to the Hospital by Paulette Bourgeois

FURTHER READING AND PRACTICAL TOOLS FOR PARENTS AND CAREGIVERS

General Parenting

The 5 Principles of Parenting by Dr. Aliza Pressman

Cribsheet and *The Family Firm* by Emily Oster, and her website parentdata.org

Positive Parenting by Rebecca Eanes

Raising a Secure Child: How Circle of Security Parenting Can Help You Nurture Your Child's Attachment, Emotional Resilience, and Freedom to Explore by Kent Hoffman, Glen Cooper, and Bert Powell

Grit by Angela Duckworth

Raising Children Network at raisingchildren.net.au, funded by the Australian government

AAP Parenting at healthychildren.org by the American Academy of Pediatrics

Toddler Care

Caring for Your Baby and Young Child: Birth to Age 5 by Tanya Altmann

The First-Time Parent's Guide to Potty Training: How to Ditch Diapers Fast (and for Good!) by Jazmine McCoy

ZERO TO THREE early childhood development organization at zerotothree.org/resources/for-families by experts in child development

Toddler Behavior

The Yes Brain and *No-Drama Discipline* by Daniel J. Siegel and Tina Payne Bryson

The Emotional Life of the Toddler by Alicia F. Lieberman

How to Talk So Little Kids Will Listen: A Survival Guide to Life with Children Ages 2–7 by Joanna Faber and Julie King

1-2-3 Magic: Gentle 3-Step Child & Toddler Discipline for Calm, Effective, and Happy Parenting by Thomas Phelan

The Incredible Years: A Trouble-Shooting Guide for Parents of Children Aged 2-8 Years by Carolyn Webster-Stratton

Practical Parenting Tools

Sesame Workshop at sesameworkshop.org/resources to help children understand topics ranging from medical needs and healthy living to trauma and grief

Kids Eat in Color eating and nutrition resource at kidseatincolor.com and on Instagram @kids.eat.in.color

Feeding Littles eating and nutrition resource at feedinglittles.com and on Instagram @feedinglittles

Parent-Child Care (PC-CARE) Training Center child behavior resources at pccarelearningcenter.com, of the UC Davis Children's Hospital Child and Adolescent Abuse Resource, Education (CAARE) Diagnostic and Treatment Center

Big Little Feelings tools for parenting toddlers at biglittlefeelings.com and on Instagram @biglittlefeelings

Co-Parenting Relationships and Divorce

Fair Play by Eve Rodsky (for parents in a shared household)

Loving Your Children More Than You Hate Each Other by Lauren J. Behrman and Jeffrey Zimmerman (for parents who are separated or divorced)

A Parent's Guide to Divorce: How to Raise Happy, Resilient Kids Through Turbulent Times by Karen Becker (for parents who are separated or divorced)

Neurodivergence and Other Developmental, Learning, or Thinking Differences

Advanced Parenting: Advice for Helping Kids Through Diagnoses, Differences, and Mental Health Challenges by Kelly Fradin

Children and Adults with Attention-Deficit/Hyperactivity Disorder (CHADD) at chadd.org for parents of children with attention-deficit disorder

Centers for Disease Control (CDC) state-by-state guide to early intervention services, including evaluation and therapy services, at cdc.gov/ncbddd/actearly/parents/states.html

Understood for All resources at Understood.org for parents of children with ADHD, dyslexia, and other learning and thinking differences

Mental Health

Breaking Free of Child Anxiety and OCD by Eli Lebowitz

Parenting Anxious Kids: Understanding Anxiety in Children by Age and Stage by Regine Galanti

Parent-Child Interaction Therapy (PCIT) skills at pcit.org by PCIT providers who specialize in treating challenging childhood behaviors

Postpartum Support International at postpartum.net and HelpLine: 1-800-944-4773 for postpartum parents who seek support for perinatal mental health struggles

Psychology Today magazine at psychologytoday.com, including a therapist directory and other mental health resources

Supportive Parenting for Anxious Childhood Emotions (SPACE) at spacetreatment.net for a parent-based treatment program for children and adolescents with anxiety, available virtually

Mindfulness

Mindfulness apps, such as Calm or Headspace, include tools for people looking to learn more about building a mindfulness practice at any stage.

Raising Good Humans: A Mindful Guide to Breaking the Cycle of Reactive Parenting and Raising Kind, Confident Kids by Hunter Clarke-Fields

Sleep

The Happy Sleeper by Heather Turgeon and Julie Wright

Taking Cara Babies at takingcarababies.com and on Instagram @takingcarababies also offers toddler sleep support.

REFERENCES

Altmann, Tanya, and David L. Hill, eds. *Caring for Your Baby and Young Child: Birth to Age 5. 8th ed.* Bantam Books, 2024.

Andreadakis, Eftichia, Mireille Joussemet, and Geneviève A. Mageau. "How to Support Toddlers' Autonomy: Socialization Practices Reported by Parents." Early Education and Development 30, no. 3 (2019): 297–314. doi.org/10.1080/10409289.2018.1548811.

Ballarotto, G., L. Murray, L. Bozicevic, et al. "Parental Sensitivity to Toddler's Need for Autonomy: An Empirical Study on Mother–Toddler and Father–Toddler Interactions During Feeding and Play." *Infant Behavior and Development* 73 (2023): 101892. doi.org/10.1016/j.infbeh.2023.101892.

Baumrind, Diana. "Effects of Authoritative Parental Control on Child Behavior." *Child Development* 37, no. 4 (1966): 887–907. doi.org/10.2307/1126611.

Bruijns, Brianne A., Stephanie Truelove, Andrew M. Johnson, Jason Gilliland, and Patricia Tucker. "Infants' and Toddlers' Physical Activity and Sedentary Time as Measured by Accelerometry: A Systematic Review and Meta-Analysis." *International Journal of Behavioral Nutrition and Physical Activity* 17 (2020): 14. doi.org/10.1186/s12966-020-0912-4.

Colliver, Yeshe, Linda J. Harrison, Judith E. Brown, and Peter Humburg. "Free Play Predicts Self-Regulation Years Later: Longitudinal Evidence from a Large Australian Sample of Toddlers and Preschoolers." *Early Childhood Research Quarterly* 59 (2022): 148–161. doi.org/10.1016/j.ecresq.2021.11.011.

De Stasio, Simona, Francesca Boldrini, Benedetta Ragni, and Simonetta Gentile. "Predictive Factors of Toddlers' Sleep and Parental Stress." *International Journal of Environmental Research and Public Health* 17, no. 7 (2020): 2494. doi.org/10.3390/ijerph17072494.

Dadds, M. R., and L. A. Tully. "What Is It to Discipline a Child: What Should It Be? A Reanalysis of Time-Out from the Perspective of Child Mental Health, Attachment, and Trauma." *American Psychologist* 74, no. 7 (2019): 794–808. doi.org/10.1037/amp0000449.

Faber, Joanna, and Julie King. *How to Talk So Little Kids Will Listen: A Survival Guide to Life with Children Ages 2–7.* Scribner, 2017

Girard, Emma I., Nancy M. Wallace, Jane R. Kohlhoff, Susan S. J. Morgan, and Cheryl B. McNeil. *Parent-Child Interaction Therapy with Toddlers: Improving Attachment and Emotion Regulation.* 1st ed. Springer International Publishing, 2018.

Gray, Peter. "What Exactly Is Play, and Why Is It Such a Powerful Vehicle for Learning?" *Topics in Language Disorders* 37, no. 3 (2017): 217–228. doi.org/10.1097/TLD.0000000000000130.

Hirshkowitz, Max, Kaitlyn Whiton, Steven M. Albert, et al. "National Sleep Foundation's Sleep Time Duration Recommendations: Methodology and Results Summary." *Sleep Health* 1, no. 1 (2015): 40–43. doi.org/10.1016/j.sleh.2014.12.010.

Koulouglioti, Christina, Robert Cole, Marian Moskow, Brenda McQuillan, Margaret-Ann Carno, and Annette Grape. "The Longitudinal Association of Young Children's Everyday Routines to Sleep Duration." *Journal of Pediatric Health Care* 28, no. 1 (2014): 80–87. doi.org/10.1016/j.pedhc.2012.12.006.

Loth, Katie A., Junia Nogueira de Brito, Diane Neumark-Sztainer, Jennifer Orlet Fisher, and Jerica M. Berge. "A Qualitative Exploration into the Parent–Child Feeding Relationship: How Parents of Preschoolers Divide the Responsibilities of Feeding with Their Children." *Journal of Nutrition Education and Behavior* 50, no. 7 (2018): 655–667. doi.org/10.1016/j.jneb.2018.03.004.

Molfese, Victoria J., Kathleen M. Rudasill, Amanda Prokasky, et al. "Relations between Toddler Sleep Characteristics, Sleep Problems, and Temperament." *Developmental Neuropsychology* 40, no. 3 (2015): 138–154. doi.org/10.1080/87565641.2015.1028627.

National Scientific Council on the Developing Child. "The Timing and Quality of Early Experiences Combine to Shape Brain Architecture." Working Paper no. 5., Center on the Developing Child at Harvard University, 2007. https://developingchild.harvard.edu/wp-content/uploads/2024/10/Timing_Quality_Early_Experiences-1.pdf.

Powell, Bert, Glen Cooper, Kent Hoffman, and Bob Marvin. *The Circle of Security Intervention: Enhancing Attachment in Early Parent–Child Relationships*. The Guilford Press, 2014.

Siegel, Daniel J., and Tina Payne Bryson. *The Yes Brain: How to Cultivate Courage, Curiosity, and Resilience in Your Child*. 1st ed. Bantam Books, 2018.

Vaughn, Amber E., Dianne S. Ward, Jennifer O. Fisher, et al. "Fundamental Constructs in Food Parenting Practices: A Content Map to Guide Future Research." *Nutrition Reviews* 74, no. 2 (2016): 98–117.

Wakschlag, Lauren S., Seung W. Choi, Alice S. Carter, et al. "Defining the Developmental Parameters of Temper Loss in Early Childhood: Implications for Developmental Psychopathology." *Journal of Child Psychology and Psychiatry* 53, no. 11 (2012): 1099–1108. doi.org/10.1111/j.1469-7610.2012.02595.x.

Webster-Stratton, Carolyn. *The Incredible Years: A Trouble-Shooting Guide for Parents of Children Aged 2–8 Years*. The Incredible Years, 2005.

INDEX

T

U

V

W

Y

ACKNOWLEDGMENTS

Thank you to the families and clients who have entrusted me with their c over the years—your dedication to improving the lives of your children and yourselves is a constant inspiration.

Thank you to my editors, Clara Song Lee, Patty Consolazio, and Lana Barnes, for the opportunity to bring this book to life and for your thoughtful feedback along the way. Thank you to my clinical mentors and colleagues for your ongoing guidance and collaboration.

Thank you to my village of friends and family who have supported me in my personal, professional, and parenting journeys. I am so grateful to have each of you. Isabeth, thank you for your devoted care of our children. Thank you to my parents and siblings for your unwavering encouragement, not only in writing this book, but through every chapter of my life. To Harry: I am endlessly grateful for you. Your steady support, loving encouragement, and thoughtful insights have shaped me into a better parent, partner, and person. And finally, to Caleb, Elliot, and Adrian: Your curiosity, joy, and boundless love inspire me every day.

ABOUT THE AUTHOR

Zoe Chiel, PhD, is a licensed psychologist who provides clinical care to children and parents. With a deep commitment to supporting families, Dr. Chiel helps caregivers navigate the challenges of parenting and child development by implementing research-backed strategies that foster warm, loving parent-child relationships and developmentally appropriate boundaries.

Her work bridges science and everyday life, translating evidence-based practices into practical tools that fit into families' busy routines and align with their unique values. Dr. Chiel lives in Connecticut with her husband and their three children.